Principles of Perspective

Principles of Perspective

NIGEL V. WALTERS FSIA

JOHN BROMHAM Dip.AD

WHITNEY LIBRARY OF DESIGN
an imprint of
Watson-Guptill Publications/New York

Coypright © 1970 by Nigel V. Walters and John Bromham
First published 1970 in Great Britain by the Architectural Press
Published in the United States and Canada 1974
by Whitney Library of Design,
an imprint of Watson-Guptill Publications
a division of Billboard Publications Inc.,
One Astor Plaza, New York, N.Y. 10036
ISBN 0-8230-4390-8

Manufactured in Great Britain

Library of Congress Catalog Card Number: 74-24766

First Printing, 1974

Second Printing, 1974

Reprinted 1976

Printed in Great Britain by
R. J. Acford Ltd., Industrial Estate, Chichester, Sussex

'Perspective is of such a nature that it makes what is flat appear in relief, and what is in relief appear flat.'
Leonardo da Vinci

Contents

Preface

This book is intended primarily for the student of design, it is hoped that it will be easily understood by the beginner and at the same time serve as a source of reference to the more experienced draughtsman. In the interest of simplicity, the text has been kept to a minimum and care has been taken to avoid unnecessary repetition. The illustrations have been arranged in parallel with the corresponding texts : these have been made self-explanatory and restricted to essential information. Practice in drawing the examples given and in making variations on the different themes involved, should help to make their meaning clear.

In order to illustrate the principles of perspective, without becoming involved with design, it has seemed preferable to dispense entirely with the representation of actual objects and to concentrate instead on the elements of geometrical construction alone. The regular and semi-regular solids and their duals which form part of this study, have an intrinsic beauty of their own ; they are of fixed proportions and all are capable of construction within a Cube. By confining the study therefore to the representation of these and other plane figures, the task has not only been simplified, but, disassociated from architecture and design, the symmetrical aspects of the laws of perspective and the vital role of proportion in freehand drawing have become more clearly emphasized.

The illustrations and examples described in the text provide a basis from which all other forms of representation can easily be derived. Once proficiency has been gained in drawing these figures, no difficulty will be found in transcribing them into buildings, furniture and other objects of a three-dimensional nature.

The subject has been examined from various points of view with the object of stimulating an interest in perspective in those who may have previously found the subject dull. The principles involved and their various methods of application, have been presented in a carefully considered order, so that the book can be used as the foundation of a programmed course of study. Systems of Measured Perspective have been dealt with first, in order that the student may familiarize himself with the technical terms and expressions used. This is followed by direct methods of drawing which bypass the use of a plan. Examples given in the latter part of the book illustrate the close relationship that exists between perspective, projective geometry, and mathematics.

In writing a book on perspective, decisions have to be made on the correct use of terminology, and one is divided between introducing new scientific expressions and continuing with some of the more picturesque terminology of the past. Some of the older expressions used, such as 'Terrestrial Plane' and 'Foot of the Luminary', possess vivid pictorial connotations that one is reluctant to give up in favour of the less colourful, and at times less meaningful, terms of today. But with the advance of science and the ever growing technical vocabulary that this inevitably brings about, some measure of rationalization between parallel disciplines must be sought. It is for this reason that the x,y,z coordinates of projective geometry have been used to demonstrate the traditional PP, HL and CV 'lines' of perspective. The use of these coordinates reinforces the concept of fixed reference planes, and in this sense an abstract pictorial image has been maintained.

O, Observer, has been used in preference to SP, Station Point because of its association with drawing from observation, and also because O, on plan, represents the point of origin or focal point of the visual rays. The term 'Triaxial' has been adopted to describe perspective using three axes of symmetry ; this is preferred to the expressions Oblique and Three Point perspective, which are both considered to be inadequate.

10

The x, y, z coordinates of perspective.

x = *Plane of eye-level.*
y = *Central Visual Plane.*
z = *Picture Plane.*

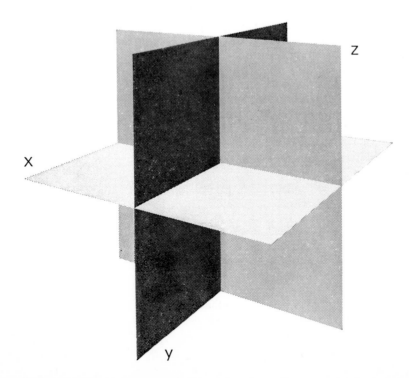

Introduction

Historical background

Realism was first introduced into painting by the use of shading and chiaroscuro techniques at the time of Pericles. The foreshortening of perspective and the divergence of visual rays was partly understood by the 4th century B.C., and fragments of the work in this style have survived in the ruins of Pompeii.

The development of perspective as a science awaited the Renaissance. Paolo Uccello (1397–1475) devoted a great deal of time to its study and is said to have exclaimed on one occasion when being called to rest by his wife 'Oh, what a sweet thing this perspective is'. His work followed that begun by Filippo Brunelleschi (1379–1446), and was further improved by Leone Battista Alberti (1404–1472), Piero della Francesca (1416–1492) and Barozzio da Vignola (1507–1573). Andrea Mantegna (1431–1516) advanced its use in figurative painting and Paolo Veronese (1528–1588) exploited its application in the form of Trompe L'Oeil. Its use spread rapidly through the invention of the printing press and the work of engravers such as Albrecht Dürer (1472–1528). Leonardo da Vinci (1452–1519), included diagrams and descriptions of perspective in his note books, and in 1499 he produced diagrams for 'De Divina Proportione', a work by his friend the mathematician Fra Luca Pacioli.

Proof of projective theory was given by Gérard Desargues (1593–1662) engineer and architect, who laid the foundations of projective geometry, and in 1640 Blaise Pascal (1623–1662) influenced by Desargues published a book on conic sections.

The beautifully illustrated 'Tractus Perspectivae Pictorum et Architecturum' by Andrea Pozzo (1642–1709) appeared at the end of the 17th century in Rome, and was followed in 1707 by the first English edition — dedicated to Queen Anne and inscribed by Nicholas Hawksmoor, Sir Christopher Wren and Sir John Vanburgh.

Perception

Perspective as perceived by man is conditioned both by his own stature and relative scale of magnitude, and by his visual perception mechanism : hence we speak of a worm's-eye view or a bird's-eye view when we refer to something observed from an unusual standpoint.

Unlike our own eyes which are able to focus only on a limited field of vision at any one time, the hemispherical, fish-eye lens of a camera has an angle of vision of 180° and is able to present the entire horizon with all that it visibly contains in the form of a circle. The effect is to deform all straight lines into curves and to produce a picture with exaggerated optical distortion. Such a form of perception does not permit ability to concentrate attention on detail, and could not combine the advantages of stereoscopy compared with our own binocular vision. In perspective drawing it is assumed that observation is from a single eye or point, and the angle of vision relatively restricted ; only in this way could it be assumed that straight lines remain straight and optically undistorted.

Methods of perspective drawing

All systems of perspective stem from two basic methods — freehand drawing, and measured drawing. Freehand perspective is taken to mean a form of drawing, in which proportions are arrived at by a combination of guesswork and geometrical construction to give a close approximation of the object without the need for exact dimensions. Although draughting instruments may be used, they are not essential. Measured perspective is taken to mean an accurate form of drawing, in which draughting instruments are used, and scale dimensions taken from a plan, ground line, or height line, are conveyed to the perspective by means of Vanishing Points or Measuring Points.

Measured perspective can be an arduous task when carried through for every detail, it also presupposes that all dimensions are in fact known. The beginner is recommended to find a middle course, whereby the broad outlines are established using a measuring technique, and the drawing continued either by guesswork or by the application of simple geometrical subdivision.

Statement of problem

The initial concept or statement of the problem is of
primary importance, once this has been decided
upon, the drawing should evolve systematically.
Drawings based on similar information should look
alike, varying only in regard to quality and manner of
execution. Preconceived ideas about the appearance
of an object, should not be allowed to influence the
course of the drawing except as a guard against
technical errors. The end result may, to some extent,
be a discovery or a revelation.

   If a drawing looks wrong, it is likely that some
point or line has been mistaken for another, and the
various steps taken should be retraced until the
cause of the trouble is found. Judgement by eye
should be the controlling factor. The student is
advised to mark all lines and points with their
respective signs in order to avoid confusion. Construction lines should be kept as faint as possible,
outlines being filled in more heavily as their position
becomes firmly established. In this way the drawing
will be complete at all stages in its development, and
errors of judgement will be minimized or avoided.

Subdivision of space

It is convenient to regard space as if it was solid, so
that all dimensions are considered as equally important whether they relate to objects or to the
intervals between them ; this leads to a correct
relationship between the various parts and the whole.
Perspective drawing can be treated either as a construction built up from smaller units or as the
dissection of a larger whole, by working backwards
in this way from the larger to the smaller, or from the
general to the particular, a greater accuracy will be
obtained.

*A symmetrical arrangement of Cubes
constructed as the equipartition of a
larger Cube.*

*A central Cube extended by the
addition of a Cube on each of its six
faces.*

14

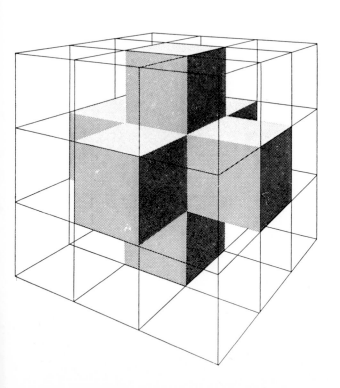
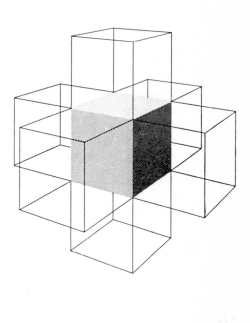

15

Fixed reference lines and planes

Two fixed reference lines are used in perspective, these are the horizontal line of the Eye Level, and the vertical line of the Centre of Vision, they provide a framework similar to the x,y coordinates of geometry, and they usually appear in the perspective drawing. Although generally referred to as lines, these may be more accurately and conveniently considered as planes observed on end. A third plane, the Picture Plane, or PP, cuts across the plane of the Eye Level and Central Visual plane at right-angles; as this is always perpendicular to the Centre of Vision, it is never observed on end as a line in the perspective drawing.

The vertical plane of the Centre of Vision passes from the Observer to the observed, providing an axis on which the object, or objects, can be rotated to produce the required view. This plane is conceived as being fixed, and the object, or objects, as being movable. In measured perspective the plane of the Centre of Vision appears as a single line both on the plan and in the perspective drawing.

The plane of the Eye Level is an imaginary plane at the Observer's eye-height, it extends from the foreground to the distance, parallel with the ground or Terrestrial Plane on which the Observer is standing. In perspective the plane of the Eye Level coincides with the Horizon Line — the visual boundary of the Terrestrial Plane, where the two surfaces appear to meet in infinity. It is therefore generally termed the Horizon Line.

The Picture Plane can be imagined as a transparent plane cutting through the path of the visual rays. In measured perspective it forms the focal plane onto which all information is projected.

The three fixed reference planes of perspective.

A cardboard or clear plastic model can be made to demonstrate the arrangement of the coordinate planes when held at Eye Level.

Plan showing position of object and Picture Plane relative to the Observer.

The Plane of the Eye Level coincides with the Horizon Line irrespective of the Observer's eye-height.

16

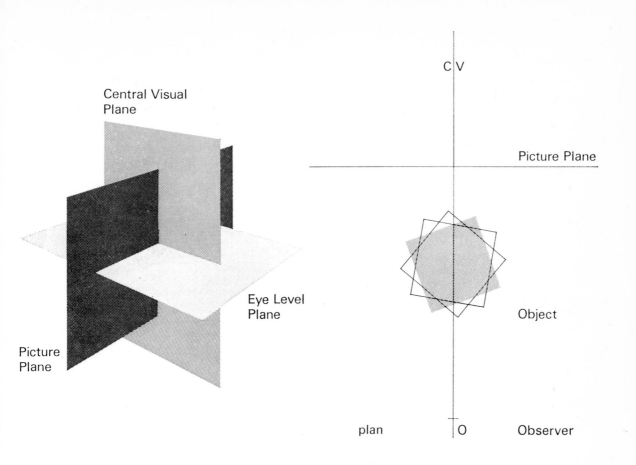

Central Visual Plane

Picture Plane

Eye Level Plane

Picture Plane

C V

Picture Plane

Object

plan   O   Observer

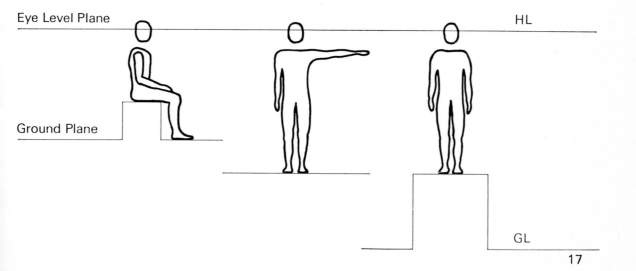

Eye Level Plane   HL

Ground Plane

GL

A fourth plane, the Ground or Terrestrial Plane, lies beneath the plane of the Eye Level. This can be regarded as being movable relative to the fixed coordinates, its distance from the Eye Level varying with the eye-height of the Observer.

Vanishing Points

Objects appear to diminish in size as they get further away, so that lines and planes which are parallel appear to converge in perspective as they recede from the Observer. Parallel lines in the Terrestrial Plane or in planes parallel with it, can be extended to meet at a point in the Horizon Line, this intersection is termed the Vanishing Point.

As a general principle, all lines which are parallel with one another vanish to the same point in perspective, and all lines vanish to points lying in the same axes as the Vanishing Points of the planes in which they occur. Parallel lines perpendicular to the Central Visual plane however, remain parallel in the perspective drawing.

The Vanishing Points for a given rectangle lying in the Terrestrial Plane, or in planes congruent with it, move along the Horizon Line as the rectangle is rotated. When the rectangle is viewed at 45° :45°, the Vanishing Points appear at their closest distance from each other. As the rectangle is turned, so the VPs get farther apart, one moving towards the CV and decelerating, the other moving away from the CV and accelerating. At the extreme position of the cycle, one VP is in the centre — at the Point of Sight — and the other is at an infinite distance away to the left or right, so that lines directed to it appear to be parallel.

Lines, parallel on plan, converging to a Vanishing Point in perspective.

Lines lying in the Terrestrial Plane vanishing to points in the Horizon Line.

Lines lying in the vertical plane vanishing to points in the vertical axis.

18

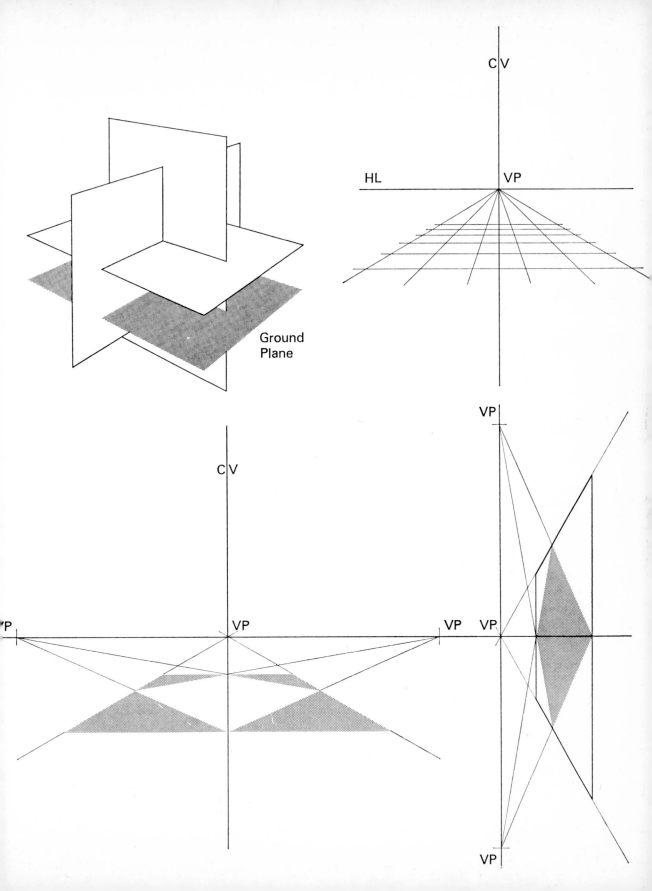

Parallel, Angular and Triaxial Perspective

Parallel Perspective

To apply the foregoing to an actual example, consider the appearance of a Cube placed centrally on the coordinates HL and CV at what is termed the Point of Sight. When the Cube is arranged square with the CV, or parallel with the Picture Plane, only one of its faces will be visible to the Observer. In this position the Cube is seen directly at Eye Level. By projecting lines from the four vertices to the Vanishing Point, or Point of Sight, and by drawing in the far side of the Cube as a smaller square, a rectangular space-frame will be constructed.

In this example only one Vanishing Point is used; all lines and planes at right-angles to the CV remain parallel, and all planes parallel with the CV appear to diminish in perspective. This is described as Parallel Perspective.

Angular Perspective

Continuing with this example, the Cube can now be rotated through 45° on plan. As it turns, the Vanishing Point will traverse the Horizon Line taking up a new position to one side of the CV, and at the same time a second VP will emerge from the opposite direction taking up a similar position at an equal distance to the other side of the CV. All lines except the vertical edges of the Cube will converge to one or other of the two VPs. This is described as Angular Perspective.

Triaxial Perspective

If the Cube is now tilted in addition to being rotated, the verticals will appear to be inclined and a third Vanishing Point will be introduced on the vertical axis. This is described as 'Oblique' or Triaxial Perspective.

All forms of perspective lie somewhere between these extremes. If additional lines at varying angles are drawn on the faces of the cube, or if additional objects are shown at varying angles with each other, then a greater number of Vanishing Points will be required.

20

The front face of a Cube arranged square with the CV remains parallel in perspective, the edges of its return faces converging to a central Vanishing Point in the HL.

When a Cube is rotated in respect of the CV its edges converge to two Vanishing Points in the HL, one appearing on either side of the CV.

When a Cube is tilted in addition to being rotated, the edges of all six faces converge in perspective. Two Vanishing Points occur in the HL and a third lies in a vertical axis.

A greater number of Vanishing Points are required when two or more objects are shown at varying angles with each other.

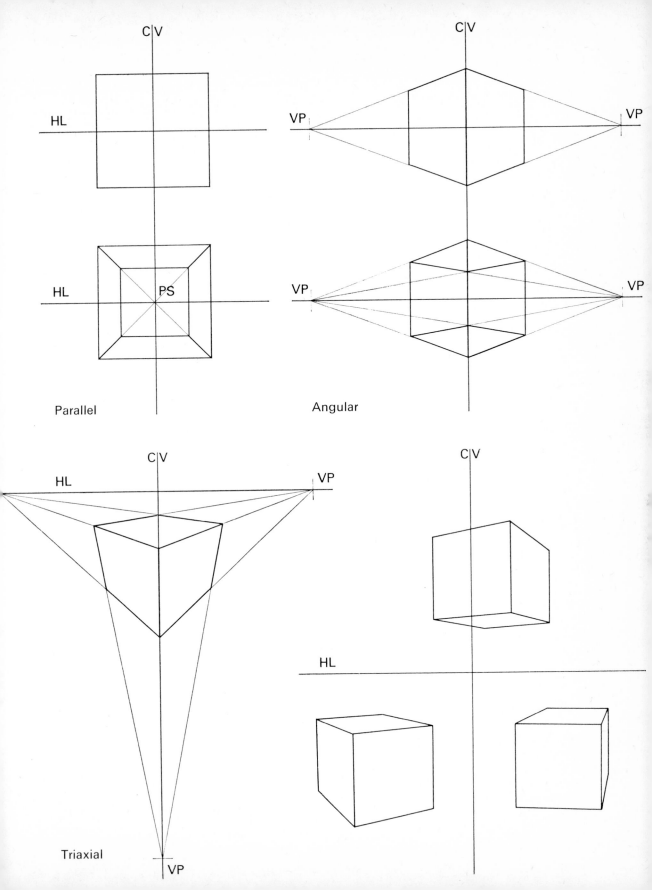

CV

HL

HL PS

Parallel

CV

VP VP

VP VP

Angular

CV

HL VP

Triaxial

VP

CV

HL

Vanishing Points appear at their closest distance from each other when a rectangle is observed at 45° : 45°.

The depth front to back of a Cube, or rectangular space-frame, in Parallel Perspective, is determined by the distance between it and the Observer. When the Observer is relatively close, the angle of vision is wide and the apparent depth greatest. When the Observer is relatively far away, the angle of vision is acute and the apparent depth diminished.

Diagonals

Rectangles of the same proportion have common diagonals irrespective of their size. When similar rectangles are arranged parallel to one another, their diagonals are also parallel and share a common Vanishing Point, or Point of Distance, in perspective. Conversely, a Point of Distance in the Horizon Line can be used to generate any number of rectangles of the same proportion at any point in the Terrestrial Plane or on planes congruent with it. Rectangles lying in vertical or inclined planes can be projected in the same way, their Points of Distance lying in the same axes as the Vanishing Points of the plane in which they occur.

Parallel lines vanish to a common point in perspective. The Point of Distance for the diagonal of a rectangle in perspective can be used to generate any number of similar rectangles lying in the same plane or in planes congruent with it.

Rectangles of the same proportion have common diagonals irrespective of their size.

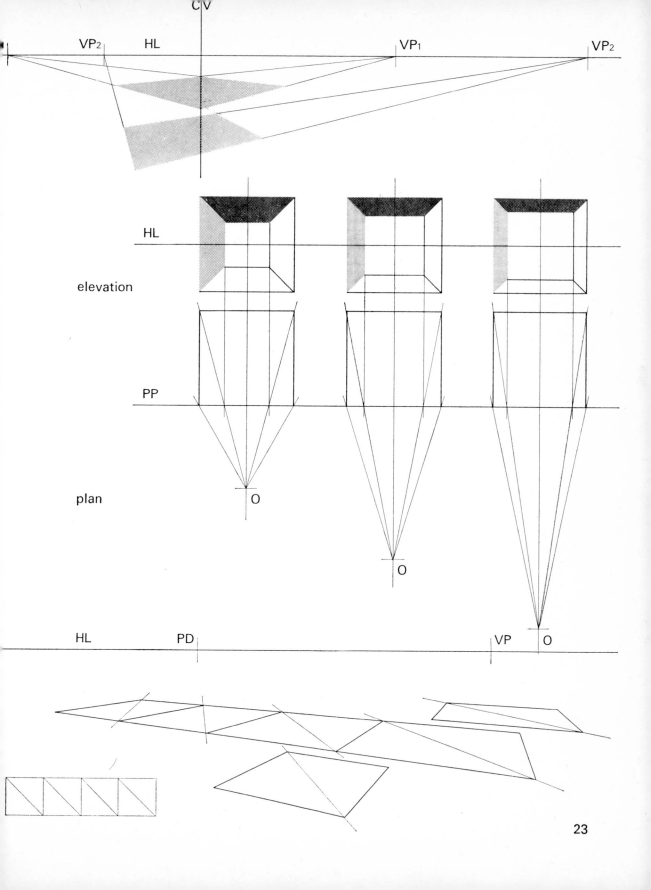

CV

VP₂   HL   VP₁   VP₂

HL

elevation

PP

plan

O

O

HL   PD   VP   O

23

Successive subdivisions of a rectangular plane in perspective, by geometrical construction.

Subdivision of the plane in Parallel Perspective

Any geometrical figure of straight lines which can be constructed on the flat plane, can be constructed in a similar fashion in perspective. The effect produced by convergence of the plane is simply to transform the figure into its perspective equivalent.

A rectangular plane in Parallel Perspective appears as a trapezium, or truncated triangle. Diagonals drawn within this figure intersect at its perspective centre, and from this the plane can be subdivided into four quarters; the process being repeated for any number of subsequent divisions. Since each set of diagonals is parallel, they converge to common Points of Distance in perspective. The four diagonals drawn from the centres of the sides of a square describe a smaller square rotated through 45°.

Subdivision of a rectangular plane into smaller units can also be effected with a scale rule. The ruler must be placed horizontally for the subdivision of horizontal planes, and vertically for planes perpendicular to the Ground. Generally, graduations must be set out on a line parallel to that which contains the Vanishing Points of the plane. Divisions are marked off and lines extended through them to meet the VP. Intersections produced by a diagonal can then be used to convert the columns into rows thus completing the regular tessellation.

Subdivision of a rectangular plane in perspective into three equal parts by use of diagonals.

Subdivision of a rectangular plane in perspective by use of scale measurements arranged parallel with the axis containing the Vanishing Points of the plane.

Units of height or width converted to those of depth by use of a diagonal.

24

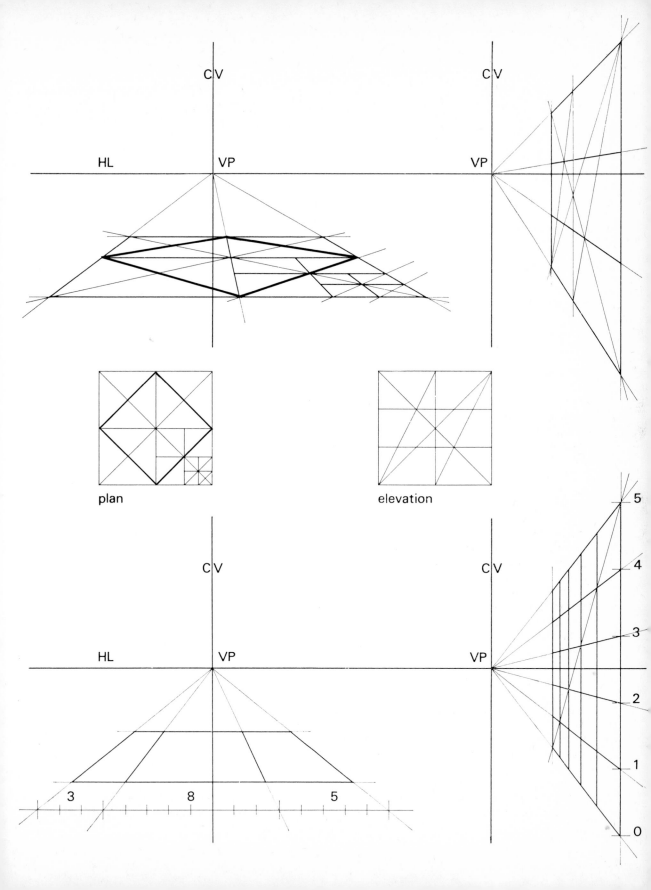

plan

elevation

CV

V

HL

VP

CV

V

VP

CV

V

HL

VP

CV

V

VP

3   8   5

5

4

3

2

1

0

Subdivision of the plane in Angular Perspective

The roles of Vanishing Points and Points of Distance are in effect reversed when a square is drawn in Angular Perspective. When the square is rotated through 45°, one diagonal becomes horizontal and the other vertical.

A square of any size observed in this way, can be constructed by setting out the diagonals as a vertical and a horizontal line ; the vertical coinciding with the CV. Vanishing Points are located symmetrically in the Horizon Line, and lines extended through them to meet the CV. A horizontal line drawn through the plane gives the depth of sides of a square. This figure has only two variables, the height of the plane relative to the Eye Level, or Horizon Line, and the distance between the Vanishing Points ; both are related to scale. The figure can be extended or subdivided by repeated use of the diagonals. The centres of sides form a smaller square in Parallel Perspective.

Subdivision of the plane in Angular Perspective can also be effected by the use of a scale rule placed parallel with the axis containing the Vanishing Points (see page 29). Units of measurement must be placed so that they fit exactly between the converging sides of the figure. Points marked off can then be used to form columns, and if required, converted into rows by the use of a diagonal.

Measurements taken in this way must be regarded simply as ratio and not as scale dimensions.

Congruent planes

Extension of a square observed at 45° : 45° by repeated use of diagonals.

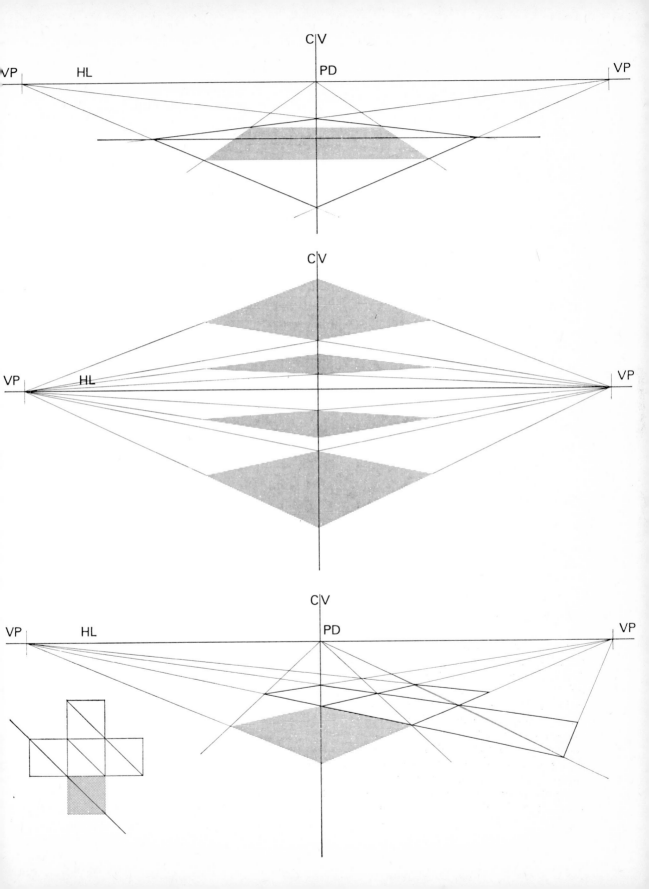

Subdivision of a plane in Angular Perspective by the use of scale measurements arranged parallel with the axis containing the Vanishing Points of the plane.

Inclination of verticals

In order to convey a true impression of scale, objects should be presented from an expected eye-height. The vertical sides of a small rectangular object appear to be almost parallel, but the sides of a large object observed from a relatively high or low Eye Level, appear to converge as it recedes from the Observer. If we look at the base of a tall building, the walls appear to be vertical ; we raise our eyes a little and the walls appear to incline inwards ; if we raise our eyes again the angle increases proportionately. In order to see the whole building at once we must stand a considerable distance away.

When the Eye Level is relatively high, or low, verticals appear to be inclined.

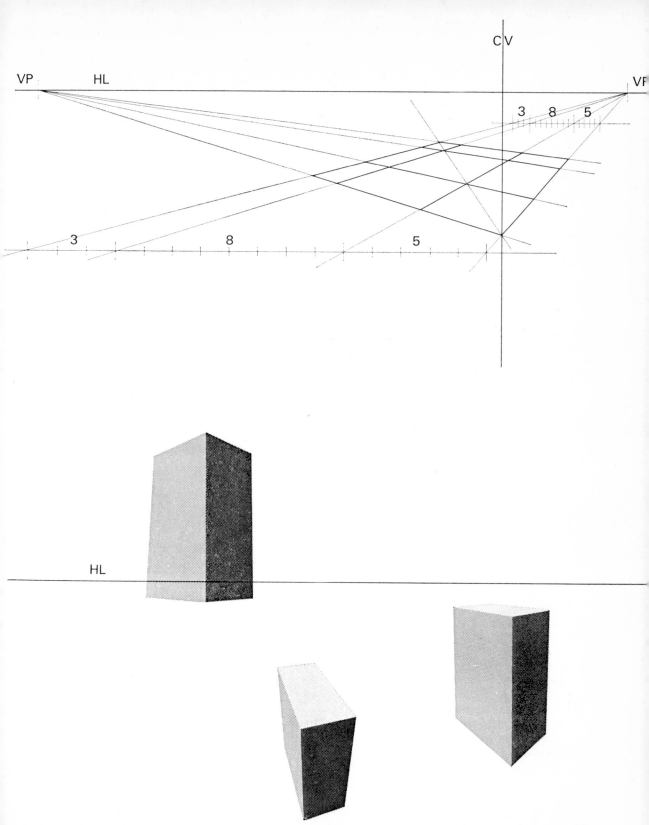

CV

VP   HL   VP

3 8 5

3   8   5

HL

29

When the Eye Level coincides with the centre of the Field of Vision, Parallel Perspective is produced on the vertical axis. When the Eye Level is relatively high or low, Angular Perspective is produced on the vertical axis.

Symmetry in perspective

We are accustomed to viewing everything from a roughly constant eye-height, and from this normal level, verticals appear to be perpendicular with the ground. As a result of this we are inclined to assume that in some way the laws of perspective operate only on a horizontal axis, but this is not so ; the laws of perspective are unaffected by orientation and behave in a perfectly symmetrical way. Rules governing the partitioning of the Terrestrial Plane, apply equally to the division of a vertical or an inclined plane, and Vanishing Points whilst commonly found in the Horizon Line are not confined to this position but may occur on similar axes in any direction above or below the Eye Level. When the Horizon Line, or plane of the Eye Level, coincides with the centre of the picture, verticals are viewed in Parallel Perspective, but in situations where the Eye Level is relatively high or low, verticals appear to be inclined thus producing Angular Perspective on the vertical axis. When the object is in effect tilted, as well as being rotated, perspective having three axes of symmetry is produced.

Triaxial perspective can be illustrated by tilting a Cube onto one of its vertices and observing it along a diagonal path. If the edges of the three visible faces are extended to their respective Vanishing Points, they will form an equilateral triangle, and produce a figure having three Horizon Lines and three Centres of Vision, or three axes of symmetry. In this example all the edges of the object are equally inclined and it has no right way up. The distance between the Vanishing Points is determined by scale, and varies with the size of the Cube relative to the position of the Observer.

A Cube tilted onto one of its vertices and observed along a diagonal path appears to be symmetrical, having no right way up.

30

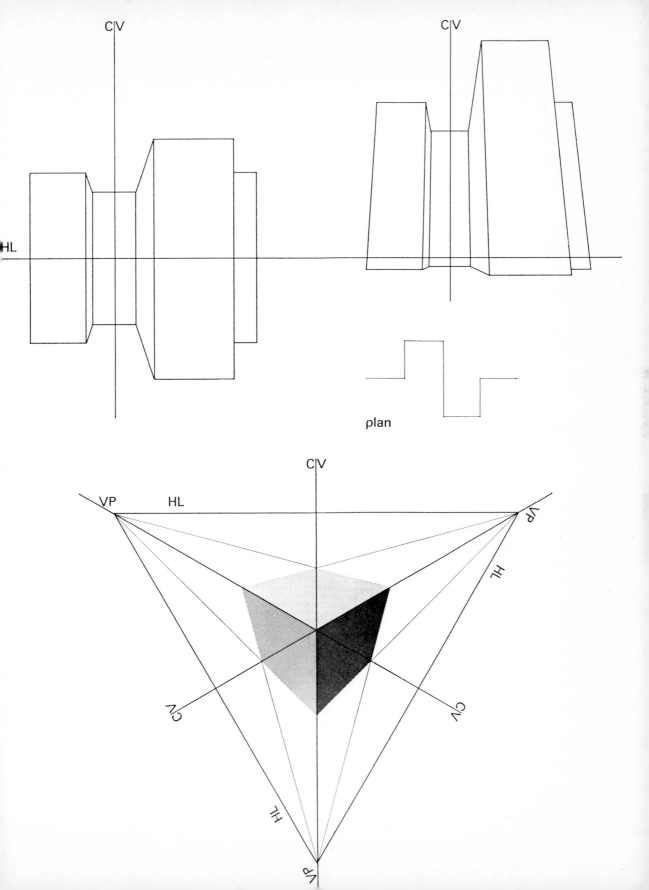

CV

HL

CV

plan

CV

VP   HL   VP

HL

CV   CV

HL

HL

VP

Field of Vision

Generally, the area of the Field of Vision in sharp
focus at any one time is comparatively small. Most
people are only able to read a few words at a time
from a line of type, and viewing at a greater distance
is subject to the same restrictions. The mind must
correlate a mosaic of endless impressions received
by the eye and assemble them into an ordered whole,
the resultant picture being reinforced by side
impressions of the out-of-focus boundary of the
visual field. The camera is able to focus in greater
depth and to some extent this is what the artist
tries to do, but there is a case as the French
Impressionists showed, for leaving something to the
imagination.

    Concentration on sharp detail in a wide angle
scene may lead to distortion around the picture edge.
Often, more is shown in a drawing than the eye
might reasonably encompass in a single glance.
This can be avoided by accepting a more restricted
view, or alternatively, by moving the Observer farther
away from the object to give the foreshortening
effect of a telescopic lens.

*The Field of Vision in sharp focus at
any one time is comparatively small.
Distortion can be avoided by accepting
a restricted view, or by moving the
Observer farther away from the object
so that the Vanishing Points become
more widely spaced. Note that the
smaller figure contained within the
Field of Vision is less distorted
than the larger one.*

*   The leading angle of a plane in
perspective at or near the CV, should
not be less than the actual angle; the
leading vertex of the square, in
Angular Perspective, should therefore
be greater than 90°.*

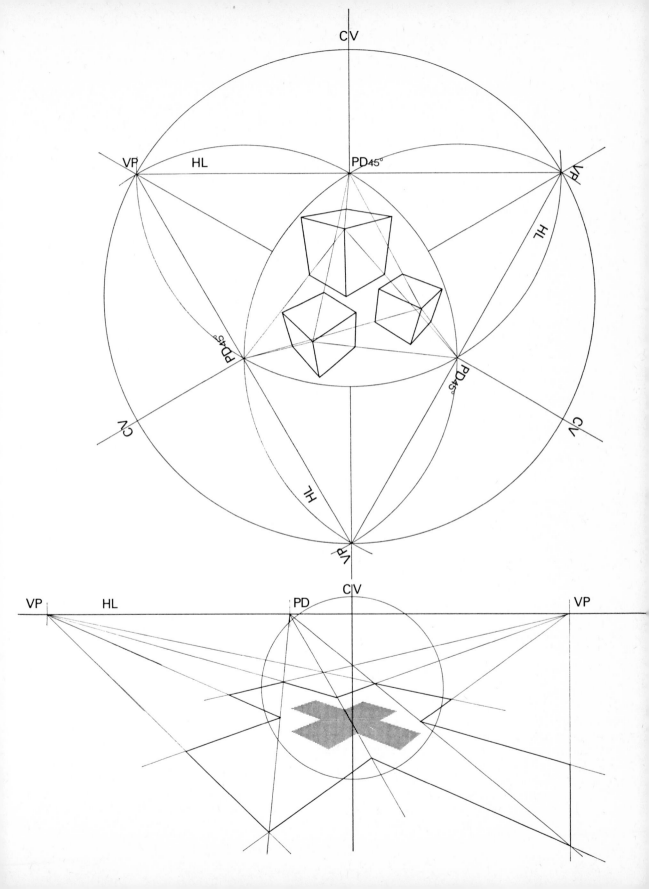

Measured Perspective

In measured perspective, information is projected on plan from the Observer at O to an imaginary screen or Picture Plane situated in front of, or behind, the object. The Picture Plane is then drawn on elevation where it becomes the finished perspective. The Observer and the object, or group of objects, are connected by the Central Visual plane which is crossed at right-angles by the Picture Plane.

The Field of Vision is defined by the intersection of the Cone of Vision with the PP. To avoid distortion, the apex of the Cone of Vision — the angle sub-tended at O by visual rays from the object's edge, should be about 40° and should not exceed 60°.

Cone of Vision

The distance between the Observer and the object is governed by the angle of vision — the angle sub-tended at O by visual rays from the object's edge. As a rough guide, the angle of vision should be some-thing like 30° or 40° but should not exceed 60°. If the angle of vision is too wide, the depth of the perspective becomes exaggerated, and if it is too acute, the perspective appears to be flattened.

Collectively the visual rays form the Cone of Vision, with the Observer at its apex, the central axis of which is the Central Visual Ray.

Picture Plane

The Picture Plane can be placed at any point on plan perpendicular to the Centre of Vision. When placed in front of the object, converging visual rays to the Observer diminish the size of the image, and when placed behind the object, diverging visual rays magnify the image. The Picture Plane can also be drawn so that it passes through the object.

When the Picture Plane is placed behind the object, diverging visual rays. increase the size of the image; when placed in front of the object, converg-ing rays decrease the size of the image

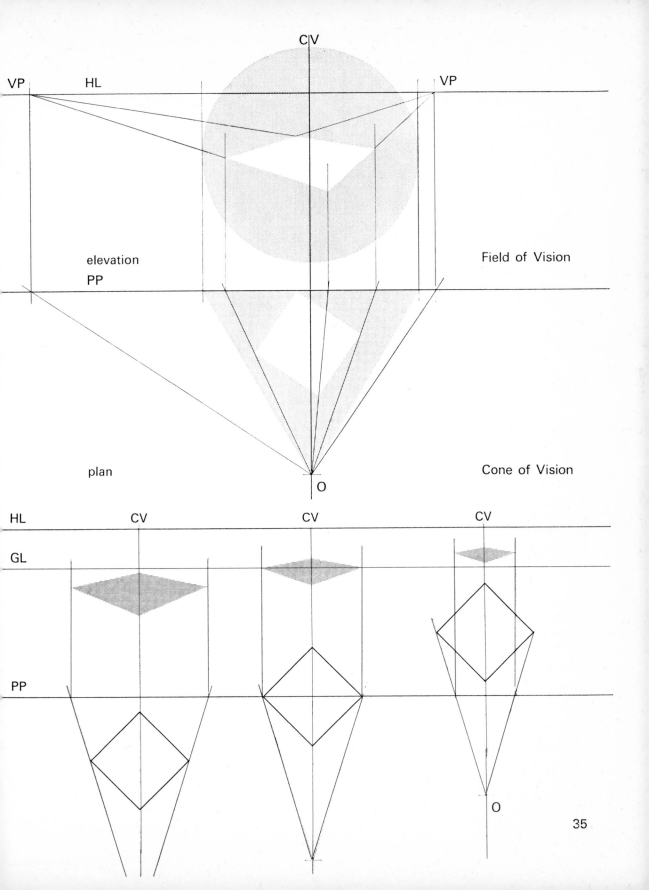

CV

VP   HL   VP

elevation

PP

                                       Field of Vision

plan   Cone of Vision

O

HL   CV   CV   CV

GL

PP

O

35

In Parallel Perspective only one
Vanishing Point is projected onto the
Picture Plane, the second VP remains
at infinity.

Vanishing Parallels

When an object is shown in Parallel Perspective, its
plan is drawn at right-angles to the CV, and when
shown in Angular Perspective, the plan is rotated to
the required angle of observation.
   Vanishing Points located in the Picture Plane, are
found by projecting lines from the Observer at O
parallel with the sides of the object and extending
them to meet the PP. These lines are termed
'Vanishing Parallels'. When the object is rectangular,
the Vanishing Parallels form a right-angle at O. In
Parallel Perspective only one Vanishing Point is
projected onto the Picture Plane, this is located in the
Centre of Vision at the Point of Sight.

Horizon Line

The perspective is begun by drawing the horizontal
line of the Horizon at any convenient distance either
above or below the plan. Space can be saved by
using the latter method, since the drawing may be
superimposed over the visual rays from O. Vanishing
Points are transferred vertically from the PP to the HL.

*Vanishing Parallels are projected from
O to the PP parallel with the sides of
the object. The points of intersection
are then transferred vertically to
produce the VPs in HL.*

36

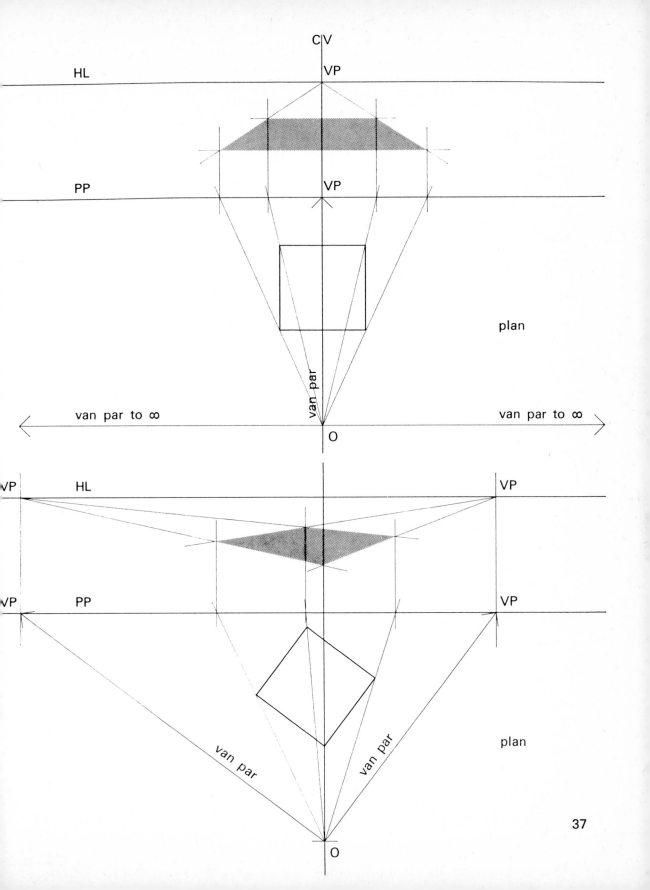

CV

HL

VP

VP

PP

plan

van par

van par to ∞   van par to ∞

O

VP   HL   VP

VP   PP   VP

van par   van par

plan

O

37

Space can be saved by placing the plan above the Horizon Line so that the perspective is superimposed over visual rays from the Observer. Care must be taken to transfer the Vanishing Points from the Picture Plane to the Horizon Line before proceeding.

The eye-height is marked off on the height line measuring downwards from the Eye Level, this gives the position of the Ground Line, or base of the PP in perspective. All dimensions remain true to scale in the Picture Plane.

Height Line

A Height Line is required to give the vertical scale, this is drawn through any point on plan where the object is intersected by the Picture Plane. Alternatively, if the Picture Plane occurs in front of, or behind the object, then one of the sides of the object must be extended to meet it, and the intersection so formed will give the position of the Height Line on plan. The Height Line is transferred vertically from the plan to the perspective.

   The Observer's eye-height is marked off on the Height Line measuring downwards from the HL, this gives the position of the Ground Line, or base of the PP. When an extension line is used to plot out the position of the Height Line, this extension line also appears in the perspective drawing.

When the object lies in front of, or behind, the Picture Plane, a line must be extended to meet it to give the position of the height line. This line will appear on both the plan and the perspective drawing.

38

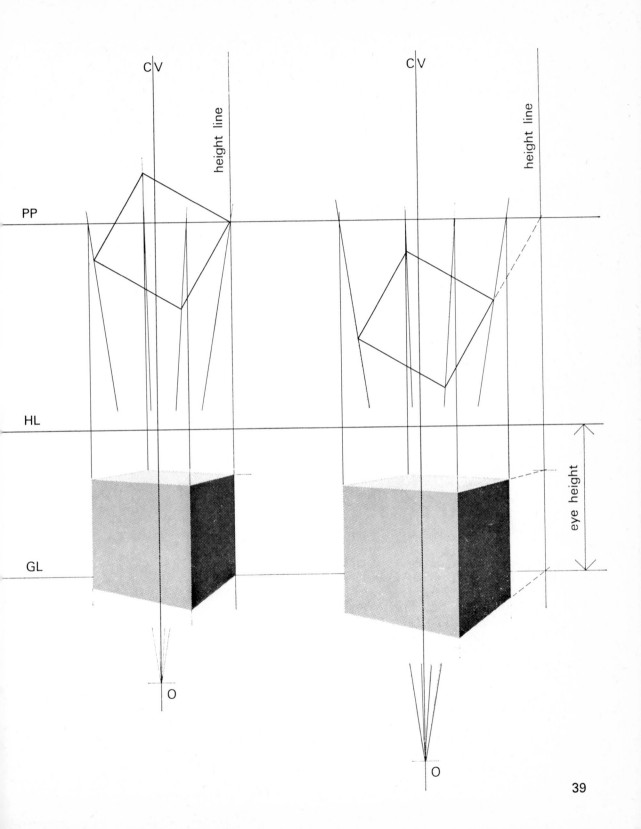

CV

height line

CV

height line

PP

HL

eye height

GL

O

O

39

All points on plan are conveyed to the PP by visual rays from O, they are then projected vertically to the perspective, and used in conjunction with radiating lines from the VPs. To avoid confusion each point should be plotted out individually from the plan to the perspective plane.

Visual Rays

Visual rays are drawn from O through all points on plan. Where these intersect the PP, they are conveyed vertically to the perspective and used in conjunction with radiating lines from the Vanishing Points. All information transferred from the plan must come via the Picture Plane. Vertical dimensions are taken either directly from the Height Line, or via perspective planes connected with it. Both Height Line and Ground Line are true to scale with the plan.

When a number of separate objects are shown, these can be linked together by lines or planes to establish their relative positions. Lines or planes in perspective, used to convey information from one point of the Terrestrial Plane to another, have Points of Distance in the Horizon Line.

The relative positions of free-standing objects on the Terrestrial Plane can be found by linking lines, or planes, with Points of Distance in the HL.

Where Vanishing Points of planes occur off the drawing, Points of Distance for diagonals can sometimes be used in place of the VPs.

40

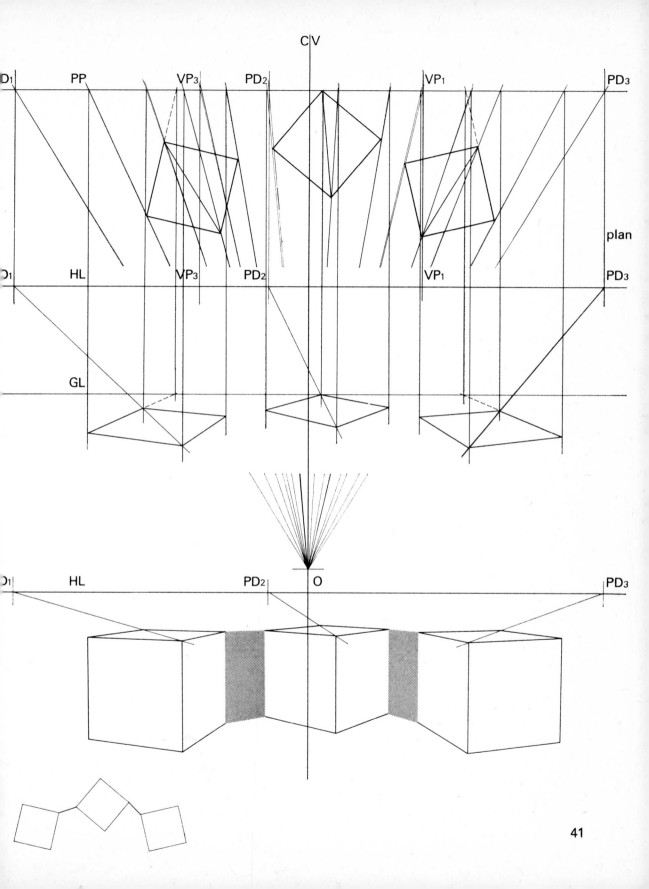

CV

For measured perspective using
Measuring Points the functions of PP
and HL are combined.
The Measuring Point is found by
drawing an arc from O to PP/HL
centred on VP. Each MP is related to
one VP only.

Measuring Points

Measuring Points are sometimes used as an alternative to a scale plan. Situated in the Horizon Line, they
behave as Vanishing Points to convey scale
measurements from the Ground Line to all points on
the Terrestrial Plane. For this method it is usual to
combine the functions of Picture Plane and Horizon
Line. Measuring Points are found by drawing an arc
from O to the PP/HL centred on each of the
Vanishing Points in turn. The eye-height is marked
off on the CV to form a Height Line, and a Ground
Line extended through its base. The intersection of
CV and GL gives the leading vertex of a plane in
Angular Perspective. Horizontal dimensions are
conveyed from the Ground Line to the perspective
by use of the Measuring Points. All measurements
taken from the left of the CV are used in conjunction
with the right-hand Measuring Point, and those to
the right of the CV are used in conjunction with the
left-hand Measuring Point. Dimensions taken from
the Ground Line relate only to the Terrestrial Plane.

*When using Measuring Points, care
must be taken to avoid confusion with
the VPs. Mistakes are most likely to
occur when MP$_1$ and VP$_2$, or VP$_1$ and
MP$_2$ are close together.*

Inclined planes

Planes inclined to the ground have Vanishing Points
above or below the Horizon Line, these points can
also be found by the use of MPs. A line at the
required angle of inclination is set out through the
MP on the Horizon Line, and extended to meet a
vertical through its respective VP. This intersection
gives the VP for the required angle in perspective.
The same procedure can be applied for finding the
Points of Distance for diagonals of vertical planes,
and for the projection of shadows cast by the Sun.
Inclined planes receding upwards away from the
Observer, vanish to points above the HL, those
inclined downwards receding away from the
Observer, vanish to points below the HL.

*The required angle α for an inclined
line or plane is set out at MP and
extended to meet a vertical through
VP, its intersection with the vertical
gives VP for the inclined line.*

42

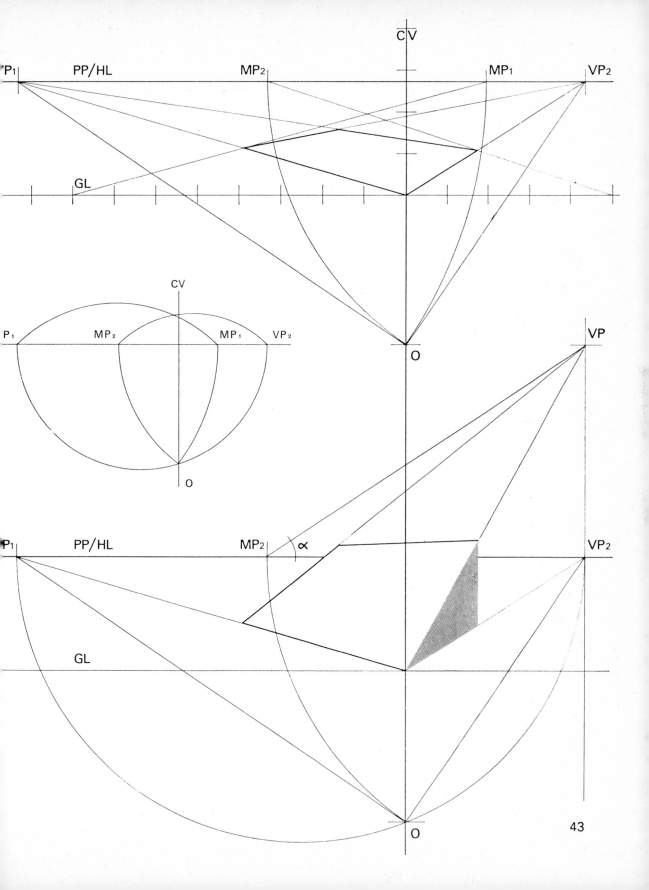

CV

P₁ PP/HL MP₂ MP₁ VP₂

GL

CV

P₁ MP₂ MP₁ VP₂

O

VP

P₁ PP/HL MP₂ ∝ VP₂

GL

O

43

Combined Picture Plane and Horizon Line

The triangular plane formed by the extended sides of a plan is in effect hinged at the PP/HL, and can be raised or lowered without changing its essential form. A PD for the diagonal can be used to draw the plan in perspective at any height, and to any scale.

When making a freehand drawing of a rectangular object, it is sometimes convenient to combine the functions of the Picture Plane and Horizon Line, as previously described. The plan serves only to establish the positions of the Vanishing Points, Measuring Points and Points of Distance, and scale is unimportant.

The plan is drawn at the required angle of vision, and the sides extended to form Vanishing Parallels giving VPs on the PP/HL. A diagonal of the plan is projected to give a PD in PP/HL, which serves to establish proportion. A CV is drawn through O. The perspective drawing can be set at any height within this field, and it can be drawn to any scale, being bounded only by a circle contained within the VPs, which sets the desirable limits for the Field of Vision.

It will be seen that the triangle formed by the VPs and O, is in effect hinged at the PP/HL, and can be moved up or down without changing the essential form of the plan. At all stages, the diagonal gives the correct proportion for the perspective rectangle irrespective of height or size.

A vertical plane can be added to the figure by drawing an elevation, to any size, at one of the Measuring Points. A diagonal of this is then extended to meet a vertical through the respective VP to give a Point of Distance. The right-angled triangle formed on elevation, is similar to that previously drawn on plan, and can be freely rotated about its axis PD, VP. The hypotenuse of this triangle establishes the height of the vertical rectangular plane relative to the length of its base. If the drawing is now turned on its side, so that the vertical axis lies horizontally, it will be found to behave in exactly the same way as the PP/HL. The position formerly occupied by the MP, serves as O, and the plane which first appeared to be in Angular Perspective, now appears in Parallel Perspective.

The angle formed by any two chords in a semi-circle is a right-angle. In perspective the chords correspond with the Vanishing Parallels of a rectangular object, the apex of the triangle being O, the hypotenuse PP/HL, and its extremities, the VPs. A perpendicular through O gives the CV.

When rotated through 90° the PP/HL becomes the vertical axis and can be used for vertical planes set out on the HL at MP.

44

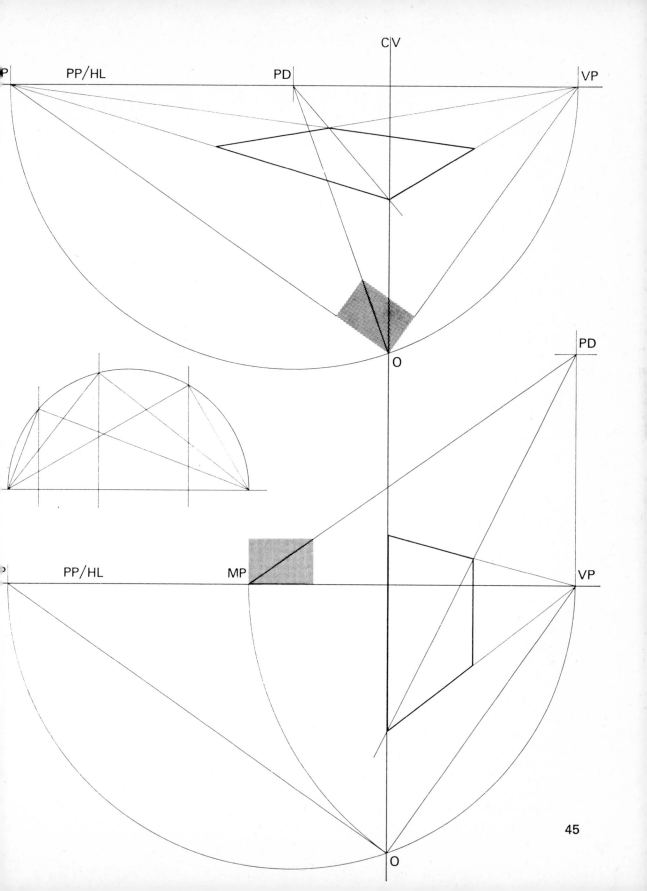

O

PP/HL   MP   VP

PD

VP

O

45

Topology

*Information from a plane, perpendicu-
lar to the CV, can be transferred
directly to the Ground or Terrestrial
Plane.*

*A number of points equally spaced
on a semi-circle can be transferred
vertically to the Terrestrial Plane and
extended to meet VP. When converted
by a diagonal from PD$_{45°}$, the transverse lines form a regular tesselation.
Successive diagonals of the individual
rectangles produce a perspective
polygon with vertices lying in an
ellipse.*

A rectangular plane and its perspective equivalent
are topologically identical insofar as the sequence of
events taking place on the surface of one, is similar
in every respect to that taking place on the other.
Perspective distorts according to the principles of
'rubber sheet geometry', so that any construction or
subdivision which is possible on the flat plane, is
equally possible in perspective ; this is true for
straight lines and for points of arcs or curves. It is this
characteristic of perspective which makes possible
the subdivision of planes into equal parts by geometrical construction, and permits the setting out of
points for the construction of ellipses.

*The topological correspondence
between a plan and its perspective
equivalent makes possible the
geometrical construction of circles
in perspective.*

46

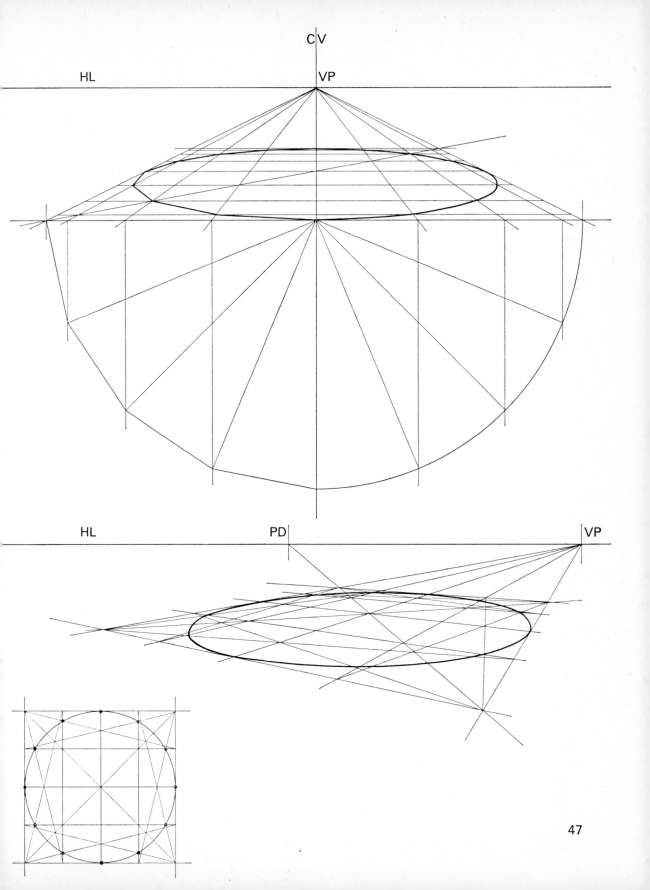

HL   VP

HL   PD   VP

47

When a square is inscribed in a circle, the ratio of square edge to diameter is 1 : $\sqrt{2}$, this remains constant for any size of circle.

Circles in perspective

A circle can be fitted into a square so that it exactly touches the centres of its sides : the diagonals of the square intersect the circle at four points describing a smaller square inside. The ratio between the edge of the inner square, and the edge of the outer square, is 1 : $\sqrt{2}$, or 1 : 1·414, this remains constant for any size of circle.

In perspective the diagram remains unchanged in all particulars except measurement. The ratio 1 : 1·414, or 1 : 0·414, can be constructed on a base line using compasses and a set-square and conveyed to the point required by means of a VP. The construction can be drawn to any scale, and at any point in the perspective. Care must be taken to see that the centre of the arc is placed on the central axis of the perspective square, and not on one of its vertices.

The ratio 1 : 0·414 can be constructed geometrically at any point in perspective, and used to determine additional points for the construction of ellipses.

48

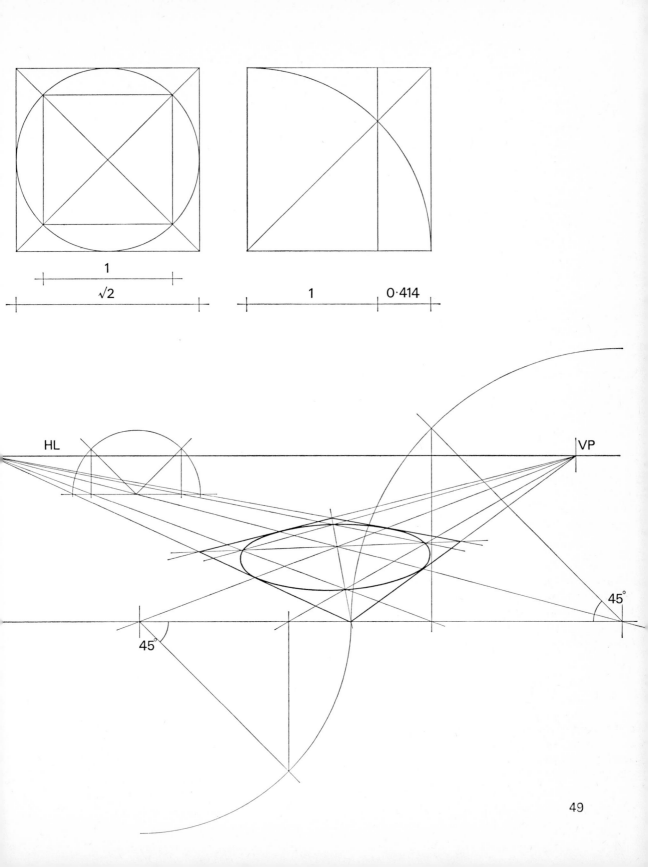

1

√2

1   0·414

HL   VP

45°

45°

49

Proportion

Perspective is closely related to proportion and the partitioning of space, and some knowledge of these subjects is of value for its proper understanding. Certain rectangles are easily recognized by their proportion, or ratio of length to side, their geometrical properties and proportional charac-teristics play an essential part in the language of design. Once the various rectangles have been identified by their respective ratios, their use will greatly assist in speedy and accurate free-hand drawing.

Ratio and proportion

Ratio is the quantitive comparison between two things of the same kind. When a line ac is divided at b, the ratio of ab to bc can be expressed in the form $\frac{ab}{bc}$. Similarly, when a line is divided into two sections of 5 and 8, the ratio of one side to the other can be expressed as $\frac{5}{8}$ or $\frac{8}{5}$. A ratio has both the appearance and properties of a fraction.

A proportion is the relationship between two or several ratios. Geometrical proportion is the special case where two or more ratios are equal, in the discontinuous form $\frac{a}{b}=\frac{c}{d}$ and in the continuous form, $\frac{a}{b}=\frac{b}{c}$ etc.

In aesthetics, the term proportion is commonly used to describe the visual effect of a single ratio, as when applied to a rectangle. Thus the 'proportion' of a rectangle can be described by the ratio 5 : 8, or 1 : 1·618 etc.

Proportional systems used in design are of two kinds : static and dynamic. Greatest order and simplicity are achieved only when one or other of these systems is adopted. In science and biology, Static Symmetry is found in the formation of mole-cules and crystals which constitute minerals and inorganic matter ; Dynamic Symmetry is found in the 'handed' molecules of organic matter, and in living organisms which alone are capable of regeneration.

50

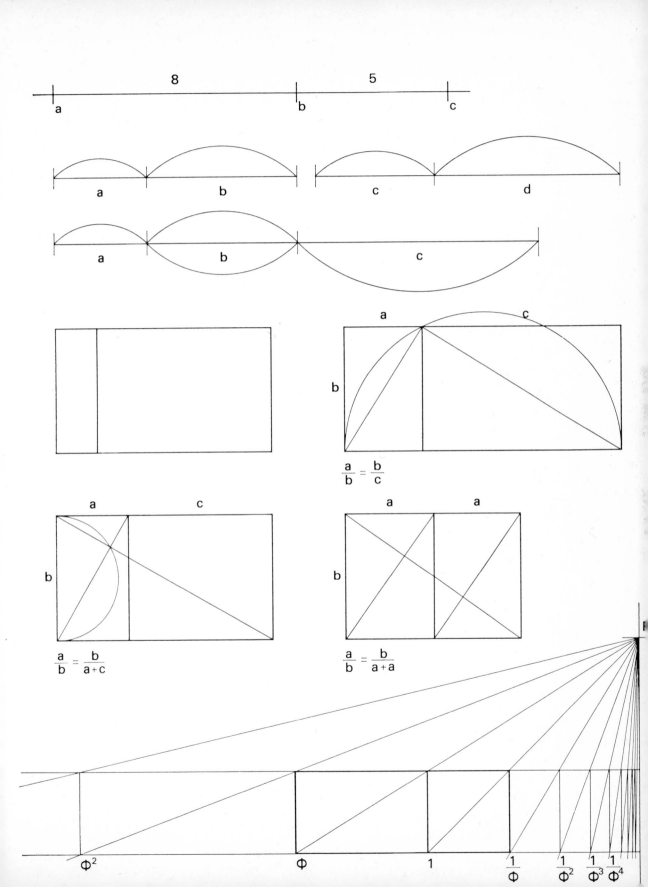

$$\frac{a}{b} = \frac{b}{c}$$

$$\frac{a}{b} = \frac{b}{a+c}$$

$$\frac{a}{b} = \frac{b}{a+a}$$

Dynamic Symmetry

Dynamic Symmetry is not static in the sense that one half of an image represents a mirror reflection of the other, yet it is in perfect balance. It is the balance of motion, or of equilibrium, and is expressed in the logarithmic spiral, in the Golden Section, and in the root rectangle.

Nature abounds in symmetry, in both the static and dynamic forms. Shakespeare has observed that the honeysuckle and the bindweed occurred only in helices of left-handed, and of right-handed, form, and that they were sometimes found coiled together.[1]

The existence of underlying principles governing the arrangement and distribution of leaves, the growth and form of animals, the development of spirals in plants, horns, and shells, and the perfect geometry of the microscopic sea creatures, Radiolaria, were thoroughly examined by D'Arcy W. Thompson.[2] He found a recurrence of the Golden Section theme in phyllotaxis, and in both living and non-living things; he found symmetry in the arrangement of globules of dew on a spider's web; and in the corona produced through surface tension, by a splash of liquid, revealed by instantaneous photography.

Every rectangle contains a reciprocal — a smaller rectangle of the same proportion rotated through 90°, which has the short side of the parent for its long side, the diagonal of the rectangle being at right-angles to that of its reciprocal. Hambidge[3] noted that the breadth of the reciprocal increases with the breadth of the parent form until it coincides with it as a square; or it decreases until both become a straight line. This led him to discover the root rectangles and their unique proportional characteristics. Examination of the root five rectangle revealed its association with the Golden Section — the area of a $\sqrt{5}$ rectangle is equal to a Golden Section rectangle plus its reciprocal, a ratio upon which all theories of proportion in architecture have been founded.

52

A total of 36 shapes is created when a square is subdivided at random into nine parts by two transverse sets of parallel lines. When the square is divided to the ratio of $1 : 1$, $1 : \sqrt{2}$, or $1 : \Phi$, the additive properties are such that it is possible to reduce the total number of shapes to as little as 4 or 5.

4 shapes
1×1
1×2
1×3
2×3

5 shapes
1×1
$1 \times \theta$
$1 \times (1 + \theta)$
$\sqrt{2} \times \theta$
$\theta \times (1 + \theta)$

4 shapes
$\Phi \times \Phi$
$\Phi \times \Phi^2$
$\Phi \times \Phi^3$
$1 \times \Phi^3$

[1] *The Ambidextrous Universe, Martin Gardner. Allen Lane, The Penguin Press, London, 1967.*
[2] *On Growth and Form, Sir D'Arcy Wentworth Thompson. Cambridge University Press, 1961. First published 1917.*
[3] *The Elements of Dynamic Symmetry, Jay Hambidge. New Haven, Conn., 1926. New edition, 1948.*

36

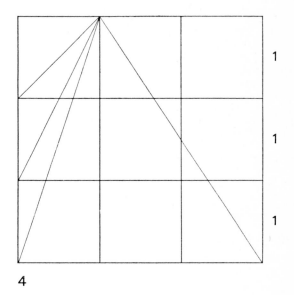

1

1

1

4

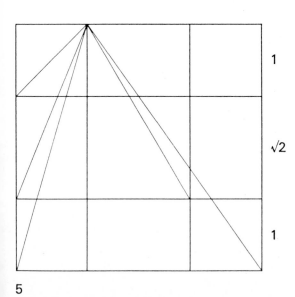

1

√2

1

5

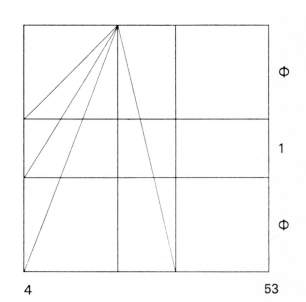

Φ

1

Φ

4

53

Golden Section

The Golden Section represents the division of a line into two unequal parts, such that the smaller part is to the larger part as the larger part is to the whole. It is a ratio or proportion commonly found in nature and it has the most remarkable geometrical and algebraical properties. The construction of the Golden Section was known to the ancient civilizations of Greece and Egypt, who attributed to it divine or mystical properties. Since that time it has been used in the design of buildings and monuments by renaissance, gothic, and modern architects. The true nature of geometrical progressions based on the Golden Number has only recently been recognized; the symbol Φ (phi) was designated by Mark Barr, after Phidias the Greek sculptor, and its algebraical expression fully developed by William Schooling.[1] Contrary to former belief the properties of the Golden Number are not entirely unique, but it represents the first and most versatile example of the family of numbers which can be expressed in the form

$$\frac{a + \sqrt{(a^2 + 4)}}{2}$$ where 'a' is a positive whole number.[2]

From this can be obtained the familiar equation

$$\Phi = \frac{\sqrt{5} + 1}{2} = 1.61803398875. \ldots$$

The Golden Section can be expressed as the continuous proportion $a/b = b/(a + b)$ or $ab/bc = bc/ac$; it forms the only geometrical progression in which any two successive terms can be added together to produce the next term. Using Schooling's notation, successive terms in the series can be expressed

$1, \Phi, \Phi^2, \Phi^3, \Phi^4 \ldots$ or in the diminishing form $1, \dfrac{1}{\Phi}$,

$\dfrac{1}{\Phi^2}, \dfrac{1}{\Phi^3}, \dfrac{1}{\Phi^4} \ldots$ For any three consecutive terms $ac = b^2$.

The Golden Section rectangle has the short side 1 and the long side Φ, it can be constructed geometrically from a square by dropping a semi-diagonal to the base and erecting a perpendicular. The ratio Φ can also be constructed from a root four rectangle, or double square, by marking off the length of the short side onto a diagonal and transferring the remainder to the base. The Φ rectangle is the only rectangle having a square for its gnomon, that is to say, a square can be added to its long side, or subtracted from its short side, without altering its proportion.

54

Construction of the Golden Section ratio from the $\sqrt{4}$ rectangle (double square).

$$\frac{b}{a} = \frac{a}{a + b} = \frac{1}{\Phi}$$

Harmonic decomposition of the Golden Section rectangle to produce the spiral of 'whirling squares'.

Construction of the Golden Section rectangle from the semi-diagonal of a square.

Harmonic decomposition of the Sublime Triangle or Triangle of the Pentalpha, to produce the geometrical progression of Phi.

Construction of the Pentagon from the $\sqrt{5}$ rectangle. The ratio of edge to chord of the Pentagon is $1 : \Phi$.

Harmonic decomposition of the Pentagon to produce the Star Pentagon, Pentagram, or Pentalpha. Continued subdivision of the Pentagram produces the geometrical progression of Phi.

[1] *The Curves of Life, Sir Theodore Cook. London, 1914.*
[2] *The Theory of Proportion in Architecture, P. H. Scholfield. Cambridge University Press, 1958.*

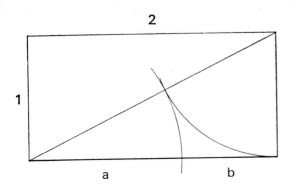

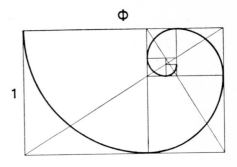

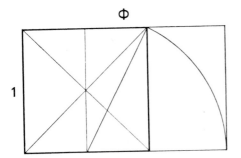

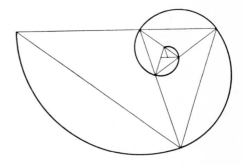

Triangle of the Pentalpha

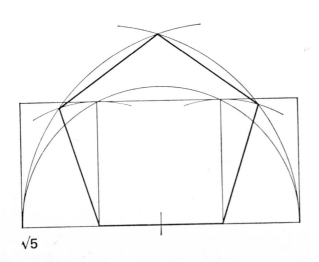

√5

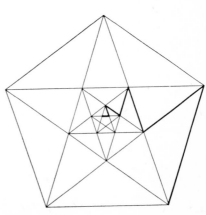

Pentagram

Subdivision of the square to produce squares and Φ rectangles corresponding with coefficients from the Fibonacci series, 1, 1, 2, 3, 5, 8, 13, 21. . . . For any three successive terms $a + b = c$, and $ac = b^2 \pm 1$. The ratios of successive terms alternate between a greater, and lesser, amount than $1 : \Phi$, the difference diminishing as the series progresses.

In two dimensions the Golden Section is related to the regular Pentagon and Star Pentagon, chord/edge; and Decagon, radius/edge; and in three dimensions to the Icosahedron, diameter of intersphere/edge; the Dodecahedron, diameter of intersphere + 1/edge; and the Rhombic Triacontahedron, ratio of face diagonals.

Fibonacci Series

The Fibonacci Series is a summation series of whole integers closely related to the geometrical progression of Φ and is thought to have been known to the Moslem astronomer and poet Omar Khayyam. The series was first recorded in Europe in the 13th century by the traveller and mathematician Leonardo de Pisa, called Fibonacci, its full significance however, was not thoroughly understood until the French number theorist Édouard Lucas[1] made an investigation in the 19th century.

Any term in the series is the sum of the two preceding terms, and for any three consecutive terms, $ac = b^2 \pm 1$.

1 1 2 3 5 8 13 21 34 55 89. . . .

As the terms in the series get higher, so their successive ratios approximate more closely to Φ, until they become accurate to three or more places of decimals.

$$\frac{5}{3} = 1 \cdot 666, \frac{8}{5} = 1 \cdot 600, \frac{13}{8} = 1 \cdot 625,$$

$$\frac{21}{13} = 1 \cdot 615, \frac{34}{21} = 1 \cdot 618.$$

Subdivision of the square to produce squares and θ rectangles corresponding with the coefficients from Pell's series, 1, 2, 5, 12, 29, 70, 169. . . . For any three successive terms $a + 2b = c$, and $ac = b^2 \pm 1$.

[1] *Martin Gardner, Scientific American, March 1969.*

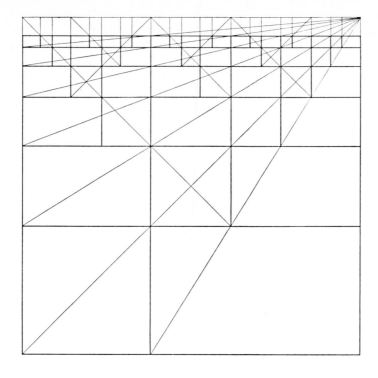

$8 + 13\Phi$ Φ^7
$5 + 8\Phi$ Φ^6

$3 + 5\Phi$ Φ^5

$2 + 3\Phi$ Φ^4

$1 + 2\Phi$ Φ^3

$1 + \Phi$ Φ^2

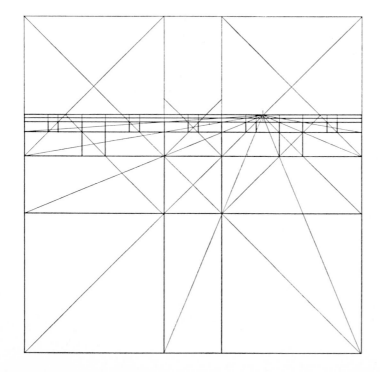

$5 + 12\theta$ θ^4
$2 + 5\theta$ θ^3

$1 + 2\theta$ θ^2

θ

Root dimensions produced by a series
of expanding arcs centred on two of the
vertices of the square.
 In the diminishing form, square roots
are generated by the intersections
produced between successive
diagonals of root rectangles with an arc
inscribed in the square.

Root rectangles subdivided into
smaller rectangles of the same
proportion.

Root rectangles

Root rectangles are so termed because the area of a
square on the long side is equal to the area of a
number of squares on the short side ; they can be
constructed geometrically from each other
commencing with a square. The diagonal of a unit
square is 1·414 or $\sqrt{2}$, this can be dropped to the base
to form a $\sqrt{2}$ rectangle ; the area of a square on the
long side is equal to the area of two squares on the
short side. The diagonal of a $\sqrt{2}$ rectangle is 1·732,
or $\sqrt{3}$, this in turn can be dropped to the base to form
a $\sqrt{3}$ rectangle. Successive diagonals of the root
rectangles continue to give the base of the next in
the series.
 A characteristic of the root rectangle is that it can
be subdivided into smaller units of the same
proportion according to its number. Thus the $\sqrt{2}$
rectangle can be subdivided into two $\sqrt{2}$ rectangles,
the $\sqrt{3}$ rectangle into three $\sqrt{3}$ rectangles, and the $\sqrt{4}$
rectangle into four, etc. The square roots of whole
integers are prominent in the regular partitioning of
space.

Harmonic decomposition of the $\sqrt{2}$
rectangle to produce a diminishing
spiral of similar rectangles.

Harmonic decomposition of the $\sqrt{5}$
rectangle to produce a Square and two
Golden Section rectangles.

Harmonic decomposition of the $\sqrt{3}$
rectangle to produce the Hexagon,
Equilateral Triangle, and the Timaeus
Triangle $2 : \sqrt{3} : 1$.

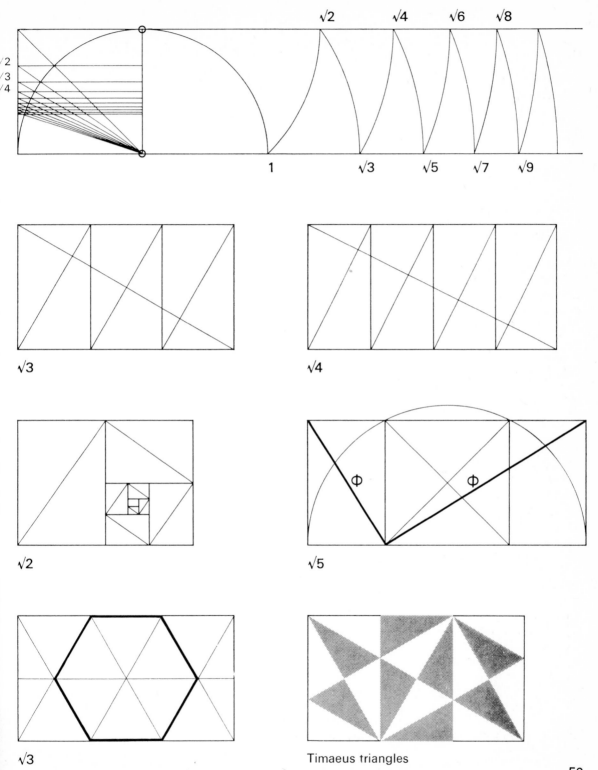

√2
√4
√6
√8

√2
√3
4

1

√3
√5
√7
√9

√3

√4

√2

√5

Φ Φ

√3

Timaeus triangles

59

Second in the family of numbers
$$\frac{a + \sqrt{(a^2 + 4)}}{2} \text{ is } \theta, \text{ where } a = 2.$$
θ (theta) = 2·414, or $1 + \sqrt{2}$
From this can be produced the geometrical progression 1, θ, θ^2, θ^3, θ^4. . . .
θ is related to the Star Octagon and to Pell's Series, 1, 2, 5, 12, 29, 70. . . .
The θ rectangle can be subdivided to produce a double spiral of 'whirling squares'.

Commensurability

Within reasonable limits, the eye is able to identify units of the same proportion compensating to some extent for the effects of perspective. The proportions of rectangles nearest to the square are most easily recognized. Beyond the ratio of 1 : 4, or 1 : 5, rectangles begin to lose their identity with the unit square.

According to the principle of commensurability, different forms of proportion, or different kinds of symmetry, should not be used together.

$\sqrt{5}$ is compatible with Φ. $\dfrac{1 + \sqrt{5}}{2} = \Phi$;

$\sqrt{2}$ is compatible with θ, $\sqrt{2} + 1 = \theta$;
and $\sqrt{3}$ is compatible with the hexagon and equilateral triangle,

$\dfrac{\text{height}}{\text{base}} = \dfrac{\sqrt{3}}{2}$.

The square, being non-directional, forms the natural basis of all proportional systems, it is commensurable with all other rectangles and rectangular solids.

Harmony is created when rectangles of the same proportion are used together, and contrast is created when dissimilar rectangles are used. Discord or imbalance is produced when rectangles of almost similar proportion are used together. Contrast, harmony and discord can also be produced by the relative scales of magnitude between two or more rectangles. Contrast and harmony are united when two rectangles of the same proportion are used in a totally different scale. Rectangles derived from a common module, may have an esoteric harmony without an obvious visual correspondence.

A0	841 × 1189	A6	105 × 148
A1	594 × 841	A7	74 × 105
A2	420 × 594	A8	52 × 74
A3	297 × 420	A9	37 × 52
A4	210 × 297	A10	26 × 37
A5	148 × 210		

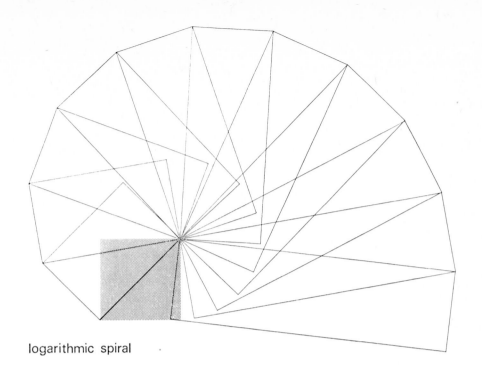

logarithmic spiral

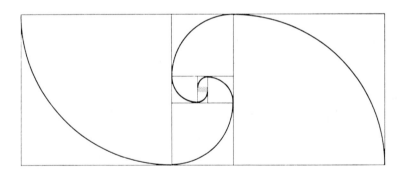

$\theta = 1 + \sqrt{2}$

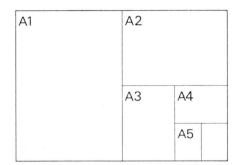

A1 A2

A3 A4

A5

A paper sizes

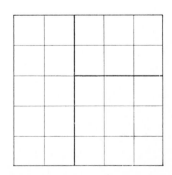

module

61

Shadow Projection

Sciagraphy

Sciagraphy, the art of shadow projection, can be applied to both measured and freehand perspective; it proceeds from the principles governing inclined planes. For convenience it is assumed that the light emitted from a point source travels in planes which are perpendicular to the surface on which they fall, the planes of light radiating from a common perpendicular axis. Rays or paths of light traverse the planes diagonally, forming a series of right-angled triangles between the source and the illuminated surface. Where the triangles so formed are intercepted by an opaque body, the light is obscured thus transforming the planes of light into planes of shade.

Due to the remoteness of the sun, its rays are said to be parallel, and shadows cast by them increase or diminish in perspective as they are cast forwards or backwards relative to the Observer. Light rays from an artificial source are not generally parallel due to the nearness of the luminary, and these are projected differently.

Sun in front of the Observer

When shadows cast by the sun lie in the direction of the Observer, the PD for the luminary occurs above the Horizon Line, its height determined by the angle of illumination or the length of shadow cast. The perpendicular on which the PD lies forms the axis of the planes of light, its intersection with the HL giving the 'Seat of the Sun's Rays' or the 'Foot of the Luminary'. Lines drawn from the Foot of the Luminary through points on the Terrestrial Plane represent the planes of light, and their extremities, obscured by the object, the planes of shade.

Lines representing the sun's rays are drawn from the PD for the luminary through points on the object and extended to meet the ground. The triangle formed by the intersection of the sun's ray with the top of the object, its corresponding point on the Terrestrial Plane, and the point where the sun's ray meets the ground, gives the area of shadow on the vertical plane. The area of shadow cast on the ground by the object is found by joining together the extremities of all the planes of shade.

Due to the remoteness of the sun, its rays are said to be parallel. The rays of light travel in parallel planes perpendicular to the Ground and converge in perspective as they recede from the Observer. The Planes of Light from the sun radiate from a vertical axis, its foot, the FTL, lying in the Horizon Line for shadows cast on the Ground.

Rays of light from an artificial point source travel in planes radiating from the source. The FTL for an artificial luminary lies in the plane onto which the shadow is cast.

The outline of the shadow is formed by the intersection of radials from PDL through all points on the object, with radials from FTL through corresponding points on the Ground.

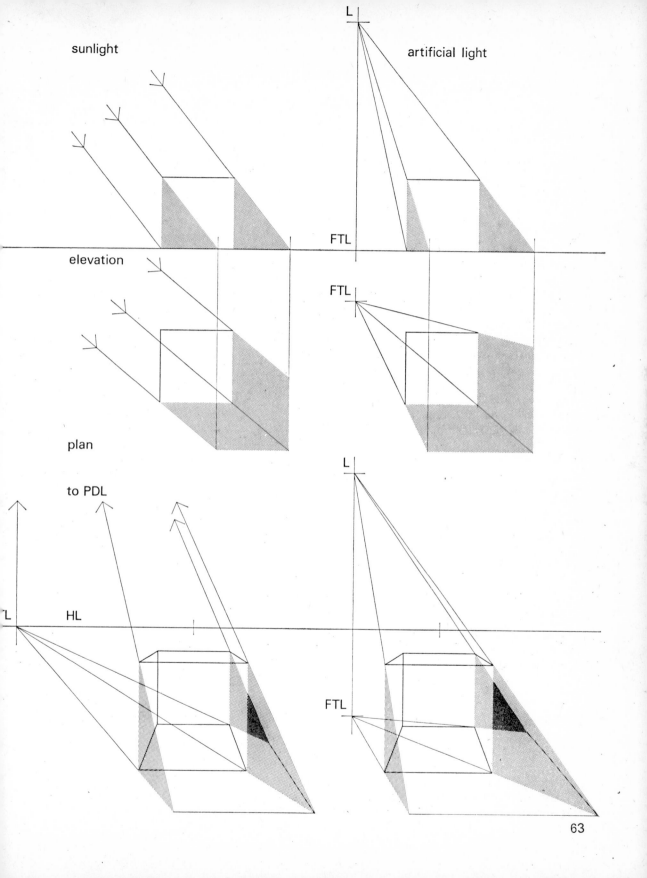

sunlight

artificial light

L

FTL

elevation

FTL

plan

to PDL

L

HL

L

FTL

63

Sun behind the Observer

Shadows cast away from the Observer are not projected from the PD for the luminary, but from the corresponding point of its pole lying beneath the Horizon Line. The position of the PD for the pole of the luminary is governed as before by the angle of inclination, or altitude, of the sun. It must be imagined that the planes of light occur beneath the Terrestrial Plane, whilst the planes of shade remain above it. In this position the FTL for the sun becomes the FTL for its pole, and remains in the Horizon Line.

It will be noticed that the vertical axis formed by the PD for the luminary or its pole, and the FTL, corresponds in every way with that used for inclined planes or diagonals of vertical surfaces, and it is to be expected that the Points of Distance will be found both above and below the Horizon Line in a similar fashion.

Sun behind the Observer.
When the sun is behind the Observer, rays of light are directed to the PD for the pole of the luminary, and not to the luminary itself.

Sun in the Picture Plane

When the sun is directly to the left or the right of the Observer, the planes of light remain parallel and at right-angles to the CV. Shadows are therefore projected in Parallel Perspective, the angle of illumination remaining constant.

Sun in the Picture Plane.
When the sun is in the PP, shadows are cast in Parallel Perspective, the angle of illumination remaining constant.

Artificial light

Planes of light from an artificial point source also radiate from a common axis, but since the light rays are no longer parallel, the Foot of the Luminary is found in the plane or planes onto which the light falls, and not in the Horizon Line.

Artificial light.

64

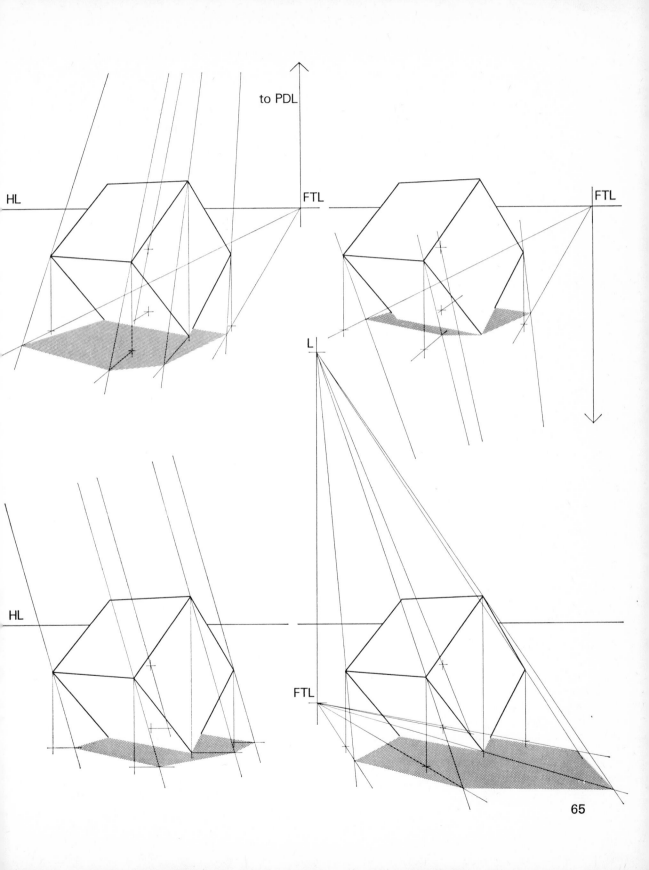

to PDL

HL   FTL   FTL

L

HL

FTL

65

*Shadow cast by an artificial luminary
intercepted by an inclined plane.
α represents angle of inclined plane.
Hypotenuse ac, of triangle abc, is
extended to give the position of FTL_2
in the vertical axis of the luminary.*

*Shadow cast by the sun, intercepted
an inclined plane.*

Intercepted shadows

When a shadow cast by the sun or by an artificial
luminary is intercepted by an opaque body, the
planes of light are redirected at the interface by a
second point, the FTL for the face of the body ;
this occurs in the same axis as the luminary and
FTL_1.

When the intercepting plane is perpendicular to
the ground, FTL_2 is at infinity so that lines directed
to it remain parallel.

*Shadow cast by the sun intercepted
by a perpendicular plane.*

66

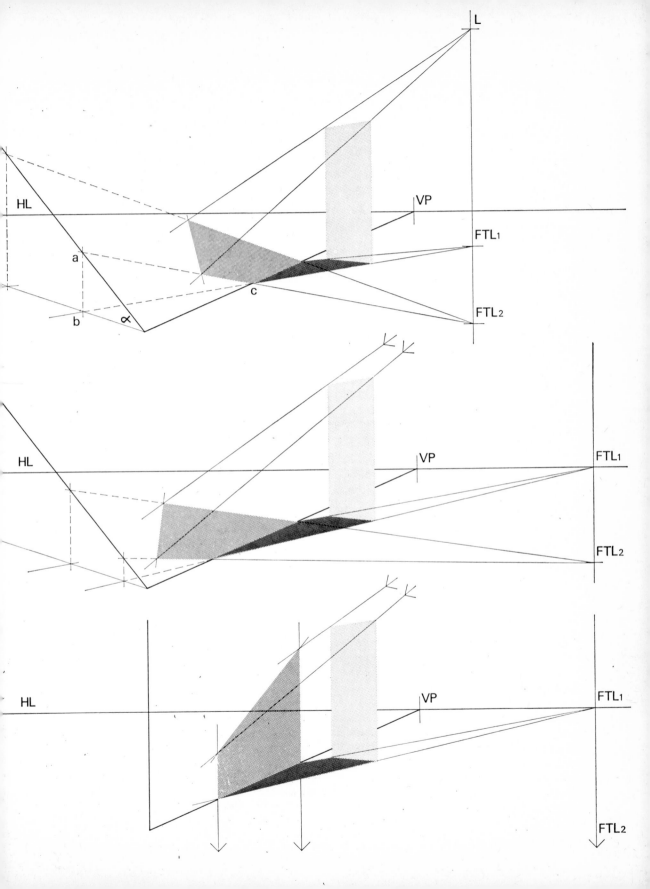

Combined shadow of two planes cast onto the Ground by an artificial luminary.

Convention of shadows at 45°

In architectural drawing, it is generally assumed that the sun is located to the left of the picture at an altitude of 45° in respect of both the PP and the CV. Shadows are plotted on the plan and elevation using a 45° set-square ; they can then be transferred directly to a perspective, or to some form of parallel projection.

Shadows constructed in orthographic projection and transferred to the perspective.

68

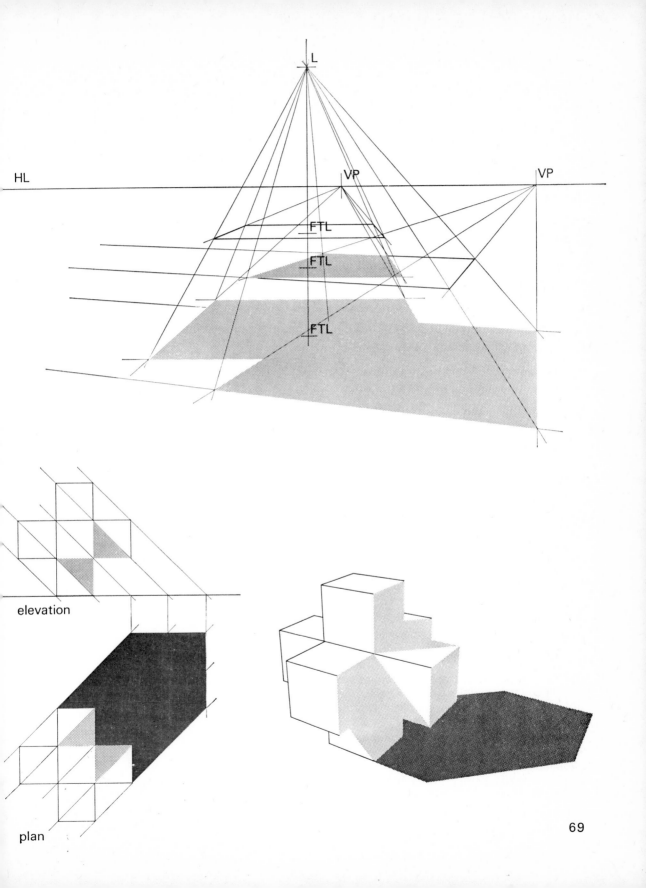

L

VP

VP

FTL

FTL

FTL

elevation

plan

69

In the example given, the shadow cast by the sun is at an angle of 45° with the ground, and at an angle of 30° with the CV.

The Cube is drawn in Triaxial Perspective, coaxial with the planes of light, and a diagonal extended from one face to find PDL. The opposite diagonal is then used to construct the inclined plane of the mediator. This plane, a $\sqrt{2}$ rectangle, must be subdivided to produce the square containing the mediator, and subdivided again to find the intersections between diagonals and ellipse. These proportions are taken from a double arc constructed on a horizontal axis to give the ratio 0·586 : 0·414 : 1 : 1 : 0·414 : 0·586. On completion of the ellipse a circle is drawn from its true centre to give the enveloping sphere, its edges touching the ellipse.

A plan of the elliptic section of the mediator is then projected on a vertical axis to the Terrestrial Plane, and from this the boundary of the shadow projected in the planes of light.

Shadows cast by a sphere

When parallel rays of light from the sun are intercepted by a sphere, the hemisphere perpendicular to them becomes illuminated. The mediator, or boundary between light and shade, thus formed lies in a Great Circle. Convergent rays of light illuminate less than half the sphere, so that the mediator formed by an artificial luminary lies in a Small Circle on the surface of the sphere.

In order to find the plane of the mediator in perspective, it is necessary to inscribe the sphere in a Cube; for convenience this is arranged coaxial with the planes of light. The rectangular plane containing the mediator can then be drawn within the cube, and from this the elliptical outline obtained. Points lying in the mediator are projected on a vertical axis to give corresponding points in the ground plane; these are then used in conjunction with radials from FTL to give the planes of light and planes of shade. Radials from PDL, through points in the mediator, give the extremities of the shadow in planes of light on the ground.

70

Elevation showing the mediator and triangular planes of shade and projected plan of the mediator.

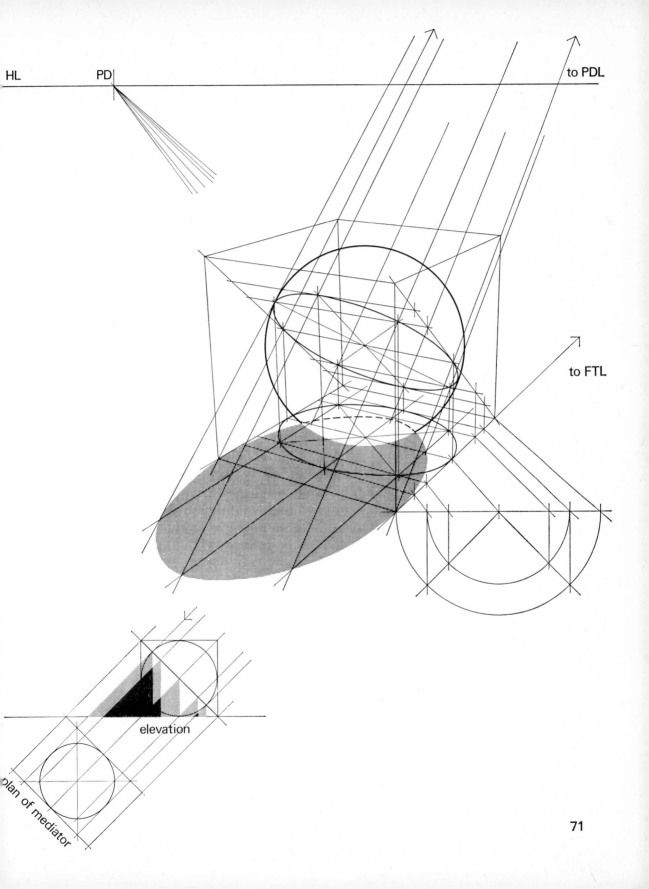

HL

PD

to PDL

to FTL

elevation

plan of mediator

Shadows cast by a cylinder

Shadow of horizontal cylinder cast by an artificial luminary.

The shadow is formed on one side by the front edge of the cylinder, and on the other side by its rear edge. Any number of points can be used to project the curved line of the shadow; each vertical has two points of intersection with the cylinder edge and can be used to produce two corresponding points on the Ground.

Shadow of vertical cylinder cast by an artificial luminary.

Any number of points can be used to project the curved line of the shadow from the cylinder edge; verticals give corresponding points on the Ground through which radials are drawn from FTL to complete the triangular planes of shade.

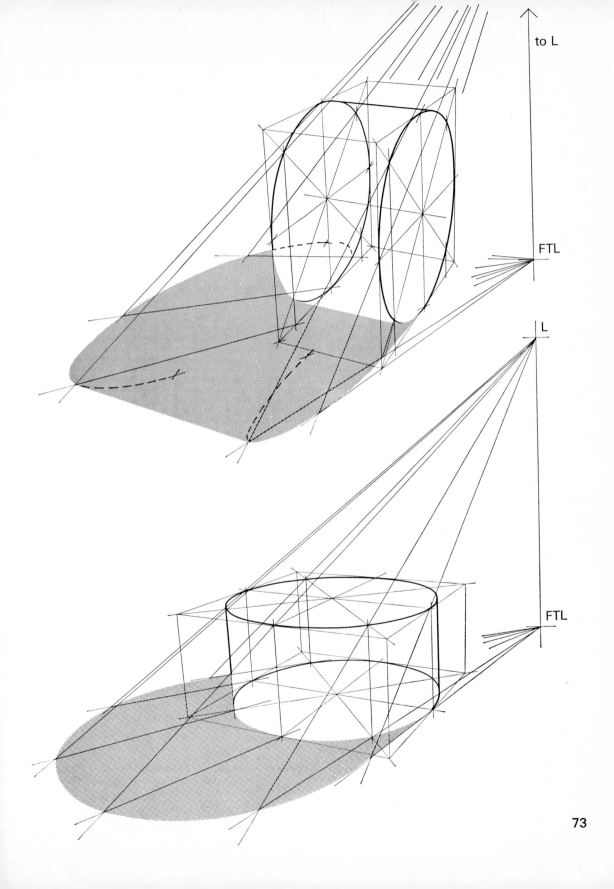

to L

FTL

L

FTL

73

Shadows in measured perspective

In measured perspective, the position of the FTL and
the vertical axis of the sun, can be found on plan by
projecting a line from O to the PP in the direction of
the cast shadow ; the point of intersection with the
PP gives the position of the FTL, this is then
transferred to the Horizon Line.
    The altitude of the sun is established by the use of
a Measuring Point ; this is found on plan in the PP
by the intersection of an arc from O centred on FTL.
The MP is transferred to the HL, and a line projected
from it at the required angle of inclination ; its
intersection with the vertical axis through FTL gives
the PD for the luminary.
    Projection of the planes of light together with the
areas of shade can be completed without further
reference to the plan.

Reflected light

The tonality of plane surfaces deprived of light is
subject to variation in intensity due to the influence
of surrounding light. Areas of shade on surfaces
deprived of direct light are usually less dark than
their shadows, since they pick up reflected light from
adjacent illuminated surfaces. Shadows with hard
edges appear to be darkest at their boundary
because of the effect produced by contrast.

*A Vanishing Parallel for the required
angle α for the direction of the sun is set
out at O, to produce FTL in PP, and the
angle of inclination β is set out at the
MP for FTL in the HL, to produce PDL
in the vertical axis.*

74

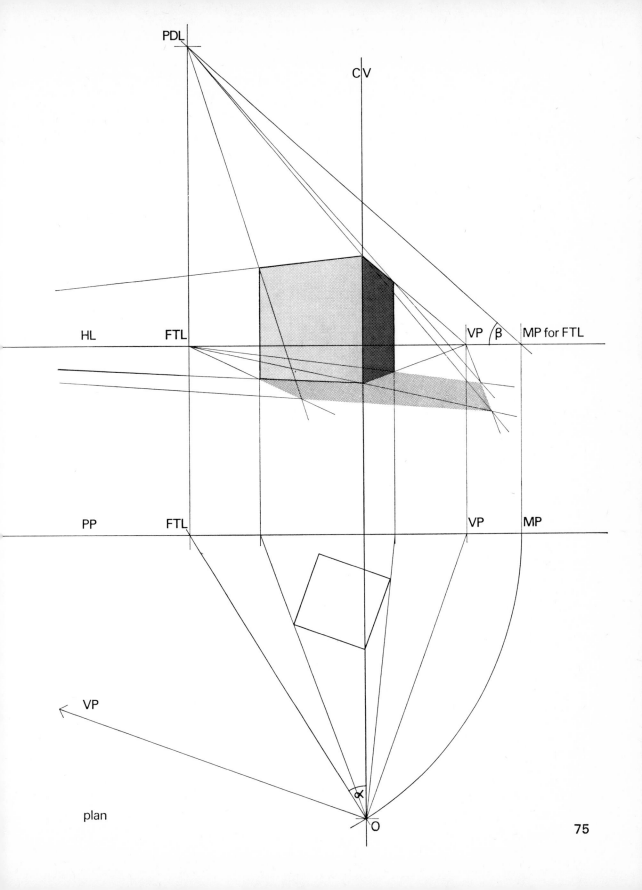

PDL

CV

HL   FTL   VP β MP for FTL

PP   FTL   VP   MP

VP

α

O

plan

75

Reflections

Reflection of a Cube in Parallel Perspective with reflecting surface parallel to CV.
The plan of the reflected object must be drawn, as if actually existing, equidistant from and parallel to the reflecting surface. Alternatively, the reflected image can be constructed directly in the perspective.

Light rays are reflected from a mirror at an equal and opposite angle to that at which they enter. Visual rays are deflected in the same way.

When the reflecting surface is parallel with the Centre of Vision, and the object square with the x, y, z coordinates, the effect is of a continuance of the Terrestrial Plane with a second object appearing in contiguous perspective at an equal distance from the reflecting surface. When the reflecting surface is inclined to the face of the object, or the object rotated in relation to it, a duplication occurs of all the respective Vanishing Points and Points of Distance. The VPs for the reflected enantiomorphic image can be found in measured perspective by drawing the reflected plan.

To avoid distortion of the reflected image, both the plan of the object and its reflected plan must occur within the Cone of Vision.

Reflection of a Cube in Angular Perspective with reflecting surface parallel to CV.
The plan of the reflected object must be drawn as a mirror image equidistant from the reflecting surface; Vanishing Parallels can then be used to find its VPs.

76

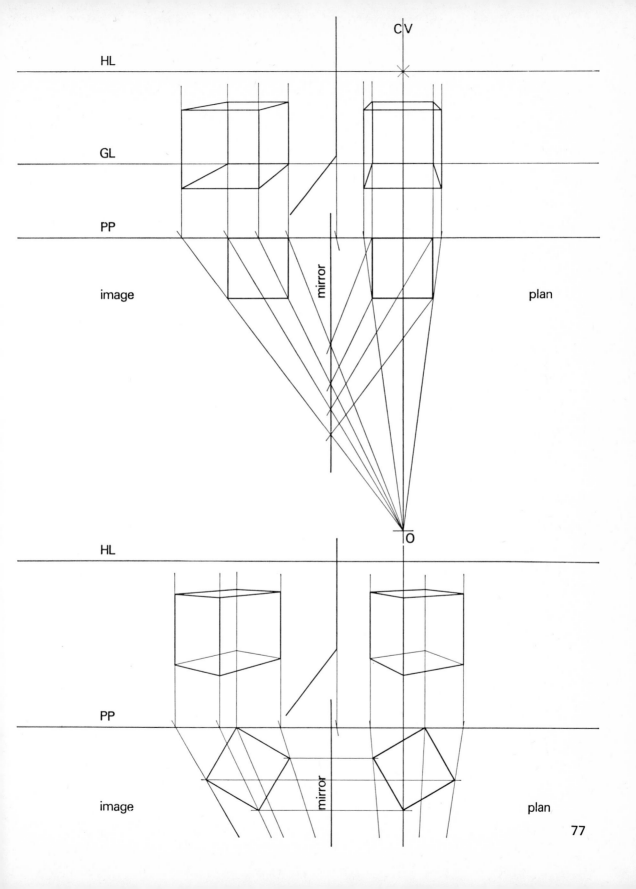

CV

HL

GL

PP

image

mirror

plan

O

HL

PP

mirror

image

plan

77

Reflection of a Cube with reflecting surface inclined to the CV.

Multiple reflection of a Cube in Parallel Perspective.

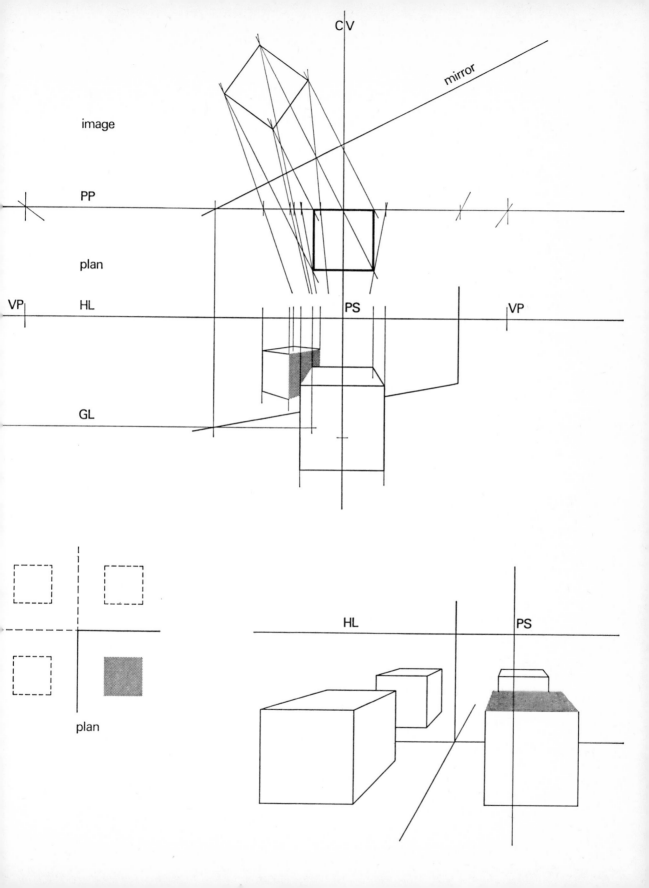

Drawing from Observation

When drawing from observation, the focal point of the object or Point of Sight, appears as its centre. Once this has been decided upon, the Field of Vision, the area of the picture in view, can be defined.

The position of the Horizon Line relative to the Field of Vision can be found from the Observer's own eye-height, this is then transferred to a corresponding position on the drawing. A centre line, representing the Central Visual plane in which the Point of Sight occurs, can be added as a guide ; its intersection with the Horizon Line gives the Vanishing Point for Parallel Perspective.

When the Horizon Line is above or below the centre of the picture, verticals appear to be inclined ; they radiate from a Vanishing Point in the CV.

Verticals are often 'corrected' and made parallel with one another irrespective of the eye position. Manipulation of the verticals in this way, either by reducing or exaggerating the natural degree of inclination, may have a tendency to destroy the true scale of the object, making it appear smaller or larger than it really is.

Principal lines can be drawn by eye, and from these the positions of their respective Vanishing Points found ; once established, the VPs can be used for all subsequent lines. Drawing should proceed from the general to the particular, detail being added as its position becomes clear.

Our subconscious knowledge of form influences our sense of perception, so that without the use of construction lines we may tend to exaggerate depth, and to underestimate the diminishing effect of perspective. The full realization of scale, and of potential drama within a composition, can only be achieved by a correct interpretation of the apparent ratio or proportion between the various parts. This is best accomplished by relating all volumes and surfaces to either squares or Cubes, which can easily be imagined and constructed in perspective, and by the use of diagonals for the subdivision of planes. Heights can be conveyed from one point on the drawing to another by means of connecting planes in perspective.

80

In drawing a group subject it should be remembered that the intervals between objects are as important as the objects themselves ; the planning and organization of the total space should be considered as a unity.

Symmetrical objects, or objects occurring in enantiomorphic form—left- and right-hand—should be constructed so that each part together with its mirror-image is set down at the same time. In this way the symmetry of the object is reflected in the drawing process, and its essential character preserved.

Light generally falls from above, so that horizontal surfaces tend to be well lit, and objects raised above the ground cast shadows beneath them. Bright sunlight and artificial light from a single source, produce shadows with hard edges ; softer shadows are produced by more general forms of lighting. Small objects grouped together sometimes share a common shadow, or pool of shade.

Tone can be used to represent either colour or shade. When applied at an early stage it serves to establish broad areas of form before exact details of boundaries have been resolved, and it becomes fully integrated in the finished drawing. Contrast in tone has the effect of coming forward, its opposite, that of receding. Realism is created when tones or colour values are expressed in correct proportion to the relative diminution of their surfaces in perspective ; non-realism or illusion is created when the tonal values of surfaces in a drawing are such that they tend to contradict the linear perspective.

As objects recede from the Observer, changes in tone and colour take place due to atmospheric density, contrasts become muted and all colours tend towards blue. This form of non-linear perspective or Aerial Perspective, as it is termed, can be traced from the 'atmospheric' paintings of the ancient Chinese and the landscapes of the Italian Primitives, through the Impressionists and the Surrealists to the present day.

A true section through any point on plan can be used as the Picture Plane; this gives the outside edges of the perspective and determines the depth of the interior.

Freehand Interior Perspective

Parallel Perspective is the simplest method of interior representation. It can be modified to produce a variety of views by moving the Vanishing Point, or Point of Sight, slightly to one side or the other without the need for altering the parallels. The end section is drawn to scale and projected either forwards towards the Observer, or backwards away from him, using a Vanishing Point in the Horizon Line.

Projection of interior in Parallel Perspective.

When the Observer is standing further to one side, the end section ceases to be parallel, and a second, distant VP is required. The VP which formerly was in the centre takes up a new position towards the nearer, and higher, end of the plane. Both the proportion of the end plane and the position of the Vanishing Points can be judged by eye. In setting out the end section, or plane, its height must be correctly related to the Horizon Line.

Modified end section to produce Angular Perspective.

The depth of the interior can be found by drawing a perspective square on one of the return planes and subdividing this to form a scale. The depth of the square is judged by eye, and a diagonal used to convert scale units of measure on one side into a diminishing scale on the other. Subdivisions in height and width can be made with a scale rule placed either vertically or horizontally at any point on the drawing, dimensions being used simply as ratio.

Rectangular space modified by additional construction in the perspective.

For the purpose of construction, irregular plans can be translated into simple forms and subsequently added to, or subtracted from, in perspective. Free-standing objects must be related to existing surfaces and projected to their required positions.

Free-standing objects related to existing surfaces to determine their size and position.

82

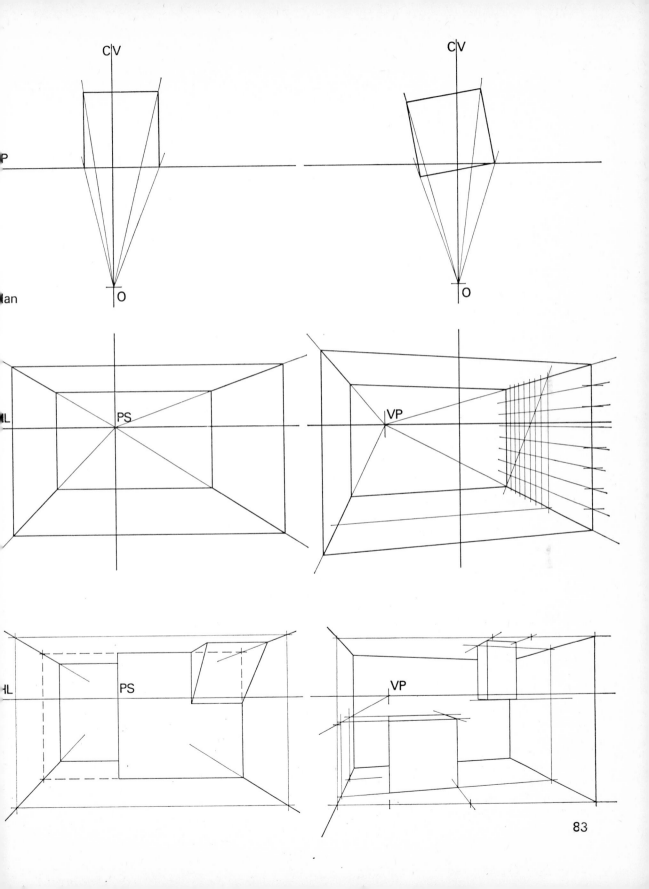

CV

CV

P

O

O

lan

L

PS

VP

HL

PS

VP

83

Triaxial Perspective

Various systems of Triaxial, or Oblique, perspective have been devised, inevitably they tend to become complex when measuring techniques are applied. The following is put forward as being the simplest and perhaps the most elegant method possible, having three Horizon Lines, three Vanishing Points, three Measuring Points, three Observers, three Measuring Lines and three Centres of Vision, or axes of symmetry, united by a common Point of Sight.

The object is imagined to be enclosed by a box, or reference frame, which is both rotated and tilted with respect to the Observer. The foremost vertex of the reference frame, corresponding in perspective with the Point of Sight, is taken as the pole of symmetry, and it can be set out to scale on the CV by measuring downwards from the PP/HL. All further dimensions are taken from Measuring Lines perpendicular to the three axes of symmetry.

As the object is tilted in addition to being rotated, the three fixed coordinate planes CV, HL, and PP, together with the Ground plane, divide into three sets making twelve in all, the CVs and GLs intersecting and pivoting at the Point of Sight. The three sets of coordinate planes continue to move relative to each other with every movement of the object.

In the special case of equilateral Triaxial Perspective, the coordinate planes are arranged symmetrically, producing at the PS a vertex figure with dihedral angles of 120°

The interpenetration of the three sets of coordinate planes creates a vastly complex system, but little of this need be used in practice, and once the bare essentials have been grasped the method can be used as simply as any other.

In Triaxial perspective the three Ground planes correspond with the top and front sides of the reference frame and not with the plane on which the object is standing. Ground Lines, therefore, have been termed Measuring Lines to avoid confusion.

The required angle of observation is set out on CV_1 at O_1 and Vanishing Parallels are projected to give VP_1 and VP_2 in PP/HL_1. PS is marked on CV_1 to give the correct height for the top of the reference frame, and lines are drawn from VP_1 and VP_2 through PS to give CV_2 and CV_3 respectively.

A semi-circle is drawn to contain VP_1, O_1 and VP_2. CV_3 and CV_2 intersect the semi-circle at points a and b. Lines extended through a and b from VP_1 and VP_2 respectively, converge in CV_1 to produce VP_3. Completion of the triangle VP_1, VP_2, VP_3, produces PP/HL_1, PP/HL_2 and PP/HL_3.

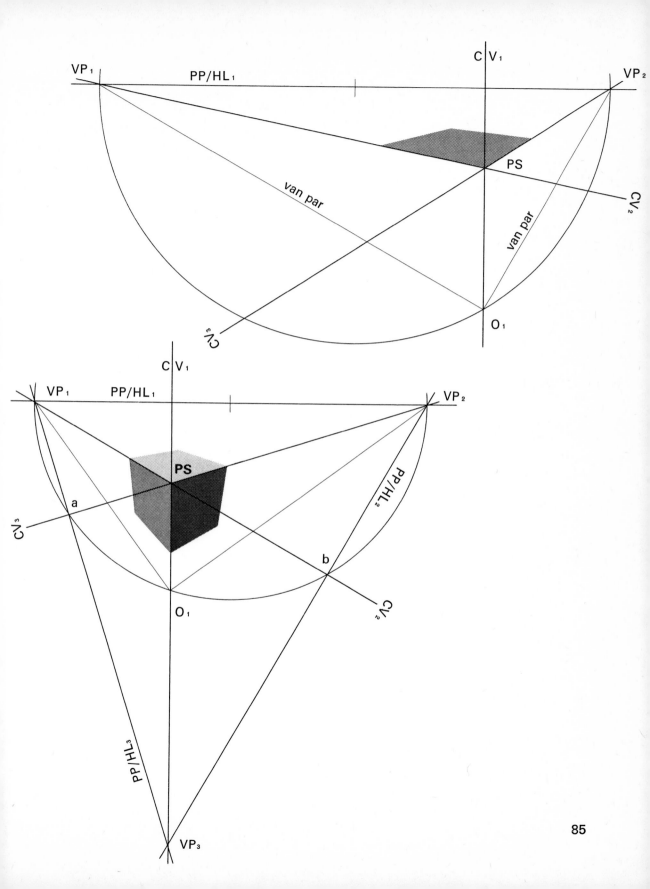

Set out O₁ on CV₁ perpendicular to PP/HL₁ and locate VP₁, VP₂ with Vanishing Parallels at the required angle of vision from O₁. Draw semi-circle VP₁, VP₂ centred on PP/HL₁ to pass through O₁. Set out PS on CV₁, measuring downwards from PP/HL₁ to correspond with distance from eye level to top of reference frame.

From VP₁ and VP₂ draw CV₂ and CV₃ pass through PS. Through intersection of CV₂ and CV₃ with semi-circle, draw PP/HL₂ and PP/HL₃ from VP₁ an to meet at VP₃. Draw arc centred on VP₂ from O₁ to give MP₁ and mark intersection with CV₂, O₂. Draw arc centred on VP₃ from O₂ to give MP₂ an mark intersection with CV₃, O₃. Draw arc centred on VP₁ from O₃ to give MF Through PS draw ML₁, ML₂ and ML₃ parallel with PP/HL₁, PP/HL₂ and PP/HL₃ respectively. Proceed as for measured perspective on each of the three axes of symmetry.

The intersection of a circle centred o with ML₁, ML₂ and ML₃, gives the lengths of edges of a Cube.

The method can also be adapted for use without measurements, serving as a means of establishing desirable angles of observation with correctly related Vanishing Points.

In the example given, only one MP has been ascribed to each PP/HL. Dimensions taken on each of the three Measuring Lines are conveyed to the appropriate plane by use of the MP. Intersections of a circle centred on the PS, with the three MLs, give the length of edges of a Cube.

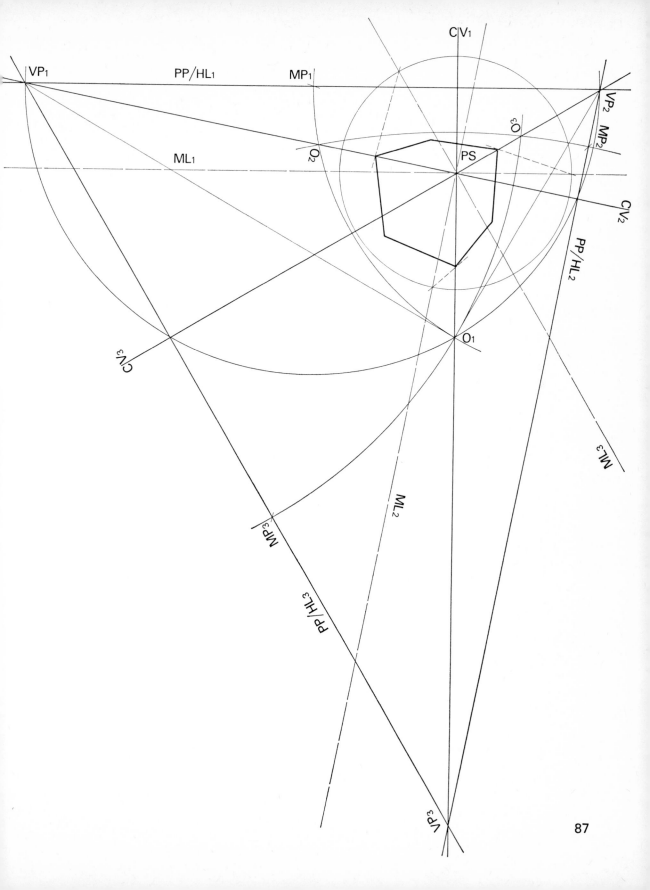

VP₁

PP/HL₁   MP₁   CV₁

ML₁   O₂   O₃   PS   CV₂

VP₂
MP₂
PP/HL₂

CV₃   O₁   ML₃

MP₃   ML₂   PP/HL₃

VP₃

87

The Point of Sight is the same vertex in each elevation observed on a different axis of vision. The variation in length of each CV is due to the varying distances between sets of Vanishing Points, and is entirely a consequence of the projection technique.

The symmetrical aspects of Triaxial Perspective are illustrated by the three half-crescents formed by arcs from O_1, O_2, O_3 to PP/HL_1, PP/HL_2, PP/HL_3 giving MP_1, MP_2, and MP_3 respectively.

Difficulty in using remote Vanishing Points, can be avoided by making the initial drawing to a very small scale. When the main outlines and subdivisions have been completed, they can be transferred and at the same time enlarged by means of triangulation, as described elsewhere.

For repeated use of Oblique or Triaxial perspective it may be found convenient to use a prepared perspective grid as an underlay. These can either be constructed as outlined on the previous page, or obtained ready-made from a supplier of drawing office materials.

If any two centres of vision are collapsed to the adjacent PP/HL, the opposite VP recedes to infinity and parallelism is restored on one axis.

Measurements taken from the three Measuring Lines to their respective MPs, give subdivisions on each face of the Cube.

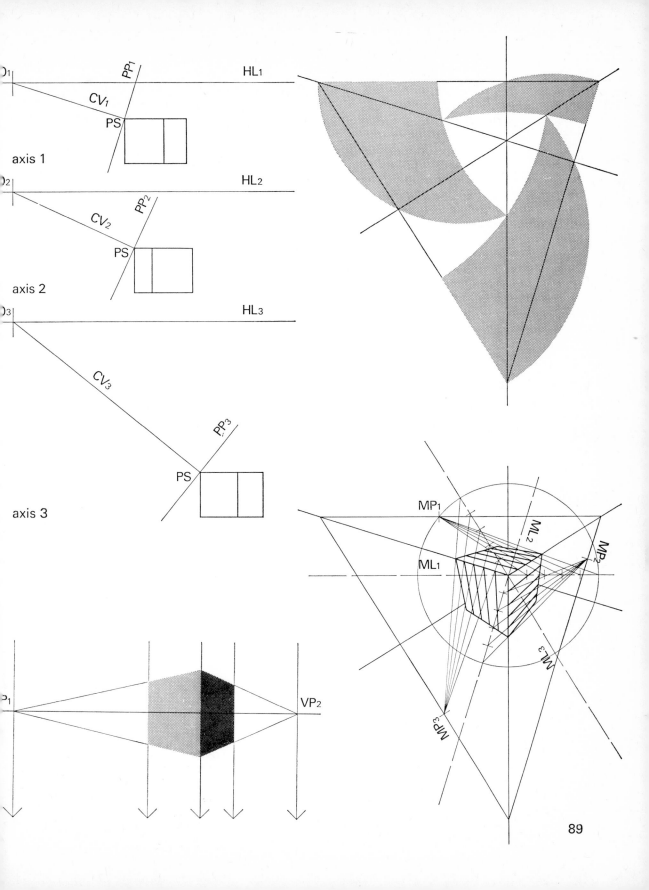

axis 1

O₁ | PP₁ | HL₁
CV₁
PS

axis 2

O₂ | HL₂
PP₂
CV₂
PS

axis 3

O₃ | HL₃
CV₃
PP₃
PS

VP₁ | VP₂

MP₁ | ML₂ | MP₂
ML₁ | ML₃
MP₃

89

Proof of Triaxial Perspective is given in the accompanying diagram in which three complete plans have been superimposed on each other; each plan represents a different face of the Cube relative to the particular axis, or CV, along which it is being observed.

The angle of rotation of each plan is determined by Vanishing Parallels from O_1, O_2, and O_3 respectively. Visual Rays from each plan to O produce points in the PP/HL which, when projected in parallel lines to the perspective, intersect with corresponding lines from points in the other two PP/HLs to give the outline of the figure. The eye-height for each Observer, relative to the particular axis, is governed by the distance between ML and PP/HL.

If the diagram is rotated in an anti-clockwise direction the Cube looks smaller on axis 2, than on axis 1, and smaller still on axis 3; it increases in size again as axis 1 is restored. This apparent change in scale is relative to the different Eye Levels, and it suggests that under certain conditions a small object observed from a low Eye Level close-to, is the same as a large object observed from a high Eye Level at some distance.

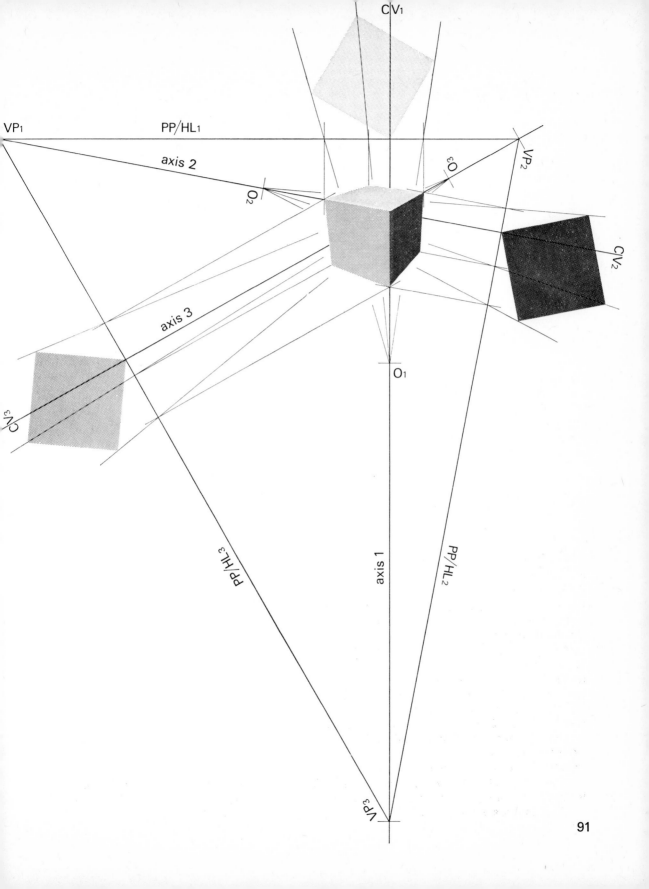

CV₁

VP₁

PP/HL₁

axis 2

O₂

O₃

VP₂

CV₂

axis 3

CV₃

O₁

PP/HL₃

axis 1

PP/HL₂

VP₃

91

Theory of Measuring Points

In Parallel Perspective, position of the MP on plan corresponds with PD$_{45°}$.

In Parallel Perspective, the position of the MP corresponds with the position of the PD $45°$. Dimensions of width taken on the Ground Line can therefore be transferred to those of depth by radials from MP in the Horizon Line to intercept lines or planes directed to the Point of Sight.

In Angular Perspective, the position of the MP corresponds with the position of a Point of Distance for the line AB, where AB is the base of an isosceles triangle formed by the side of the object, or its Vanishing Parallel, and a horizontal through O. Since OA and OB are equal, measurements taken on one can be transferred directly to the other with lines parallel to AB. The line MP, O is the Vanishing Parallel for the line AB, and MP is its Vanishing Point. In perspective, the Measuring Point serves as a VP to convey dimensions from the Ground Line O_1, B_1 to the side of the object O_1, A_1.

Position of MP in Angular Perspective corresponds with PD for line AB, where OA = OB.

92

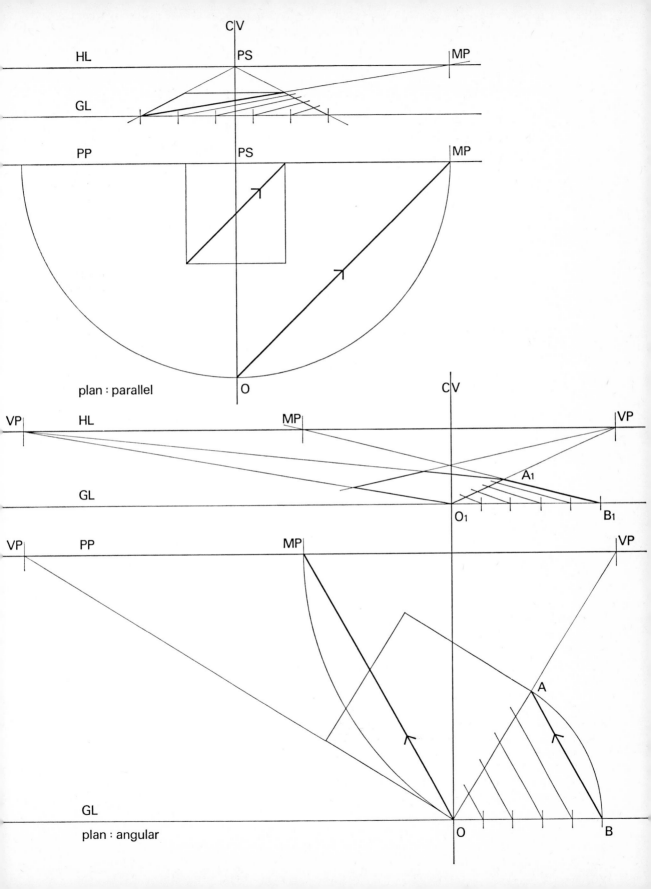

CV
HL   PS   MP
GL
PP   PS   MP

O

plan : parallel

CV
VP   HL   MP   VP
                                    A₁
GL   O₁   B₁
VP   PP   MP   VP

                                    A
GL
plan : angular   O   B

Simplified Method of Representation at 30° : 60°

Set out the Horizon Line with Vanishing Points VP_1, VP_2, at either end, and divide into two equal parts marking the centre MP_1. Divide one section into half again, to obtain the position of CV, and further subdivide the centre section to obtain $PD_{45°}$. If required a second Measuring Point, MP_2, can be obtained by equal subdivision of the end section.

A square, rotated through 30°, can now be drawn in perspective at any height and to any scale centred on the CV by using a line from $PD_{45°}$ as diagonal.

Scale measurements can be taken from a Ground Line, placed at the leading vertex of the square, using the Measuring Points.

When a rectangle is rotated through 30° the correct ratio for VP_1, MP_1, $PD_{45°}$, CV, MP_2, VP_2, is 2,000, 536, 464, 464, 536, and not 2,000, 500, 500, 500, 500 as suggested above. The method is however, accurate enough for most purposes and can be set out by eye without instruments.

MP_1, CV, and $PD_{45°}$ obtained by successive subdivision of HL between fixed points VP_1 and VP_2.

A square plane rotated through 30° drawn to any scale using $PD_{45°}$ as Vanishing Point for the diagonal

A Cube generated by a circle with radius equal to the edge of the Cube, using both Measuring Points

Relative Movement of the Vanishing Points

When a rectangular object is rotated with respect to the CV, one Vanishing Point moves towards the CV and decelerates, the other moves away from the CV and accelerates. As one Vanishing Point approaches the CV at zero, the other approaches infinity. If rotation of the object continues, the farthest VP disappears entirely from the path along which it is travelling and another VP appears in its place from the opposite direction.

Let D be the distance between the Observer and the Picture Plane. When the object is observed at 45° : 45°, the ratio between the Vanishing Points and the CV will be D : D. If the object is rotated in a clockwise direction until the right-hand VP is at 2D from CV, the left-hand VP will move inwards to $\frac{1}{2}$D. If it is again rotated until the right-hand VP is at 3D from CV, the left-hand VP will move inwards to $\frac{1}{3}$D. Generally, the relative positions of the Vanishing Points with respect to the CV can be described in the form D/N : ND, where D is the distance between the Observer and PP, and N is a positive number or fraction.

The distance between two VPs, for a rectangular object, increases as the object is rotated from a position at 45° : 45° until it reaches infinity.

$$\frac{D}{N} : ND$$

$$\rightarrow 0 : \rightarrow \infty$$

94

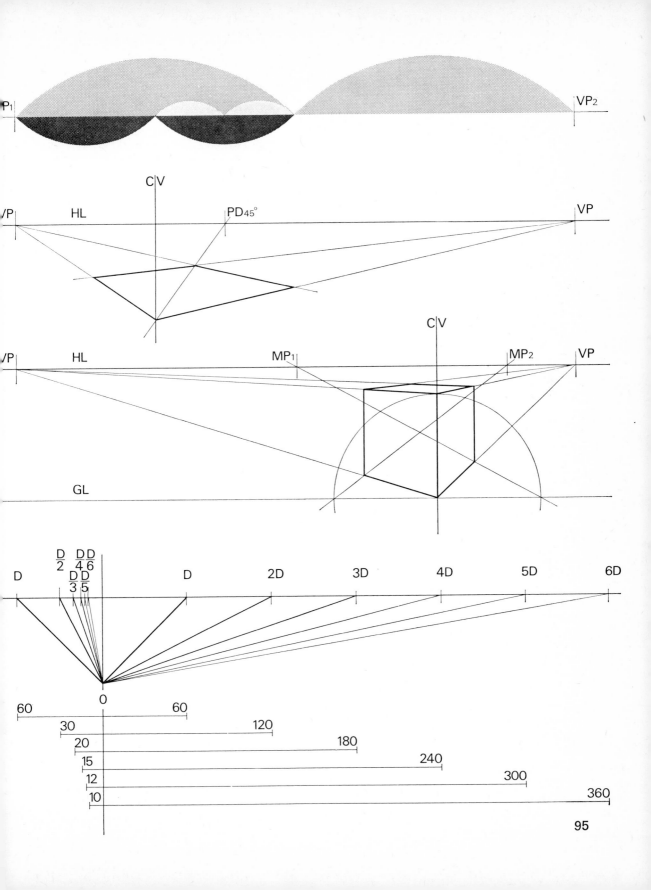

Method of Simulating Remote Vanishing Points

Lines converging to a point in HL are spaced in equal ratio at the intersection of any perpendicular.

Grid of convergent lines for use in freehand drawing.

Measurements of differing scales can be set out at either end of the coordinates HL and CV, and joined together to produce convergent lines for use as a guide in freehand drawing. The lines of measurement must be perpendicular to the coordinates, and can be moved inwards or outwards to achieve any degree of adjustment of the angles. Scales of measurement can be tried experimentally, or alternatively by working backwards from a line at a given angle — when the spaces at either end must be subdivided into an equal number of parts.

Lines drawn through corresponding points, equally spaced but of different scale, on two lines perpendicular to a common axis, converge to a point on the axis.

A Theta rectangle used to obtain the ratio of edge, to edge of containing Cube, of the Small Rhombicubocta-hedron in association with a grid of convergent lines.

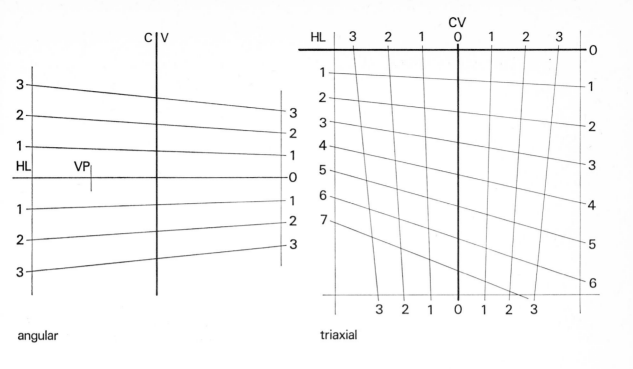

angular

triaxial

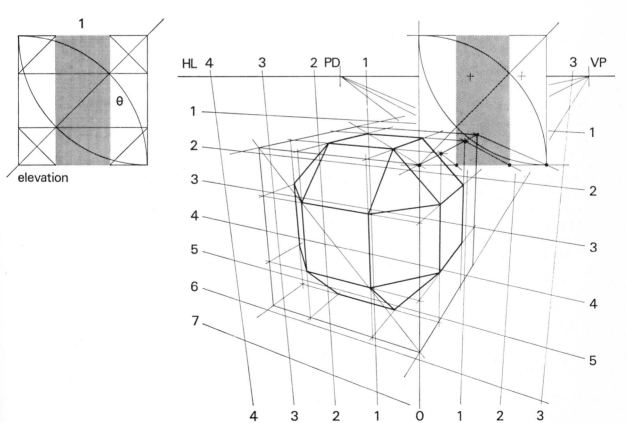

1

elevation

θ

HL 4 3 2 PD 1 3 VP

97

Inclined Lines and Planes

Planes inclined to the Ground with VP above the HL lying in a vertical axis.

All inclined lines form the diagonals of vertical planes, their Vanishing Points occurring in the axes containing the Vanishing Points of the planes in which they lie. A plane of a given proportion contains a diagonal of a given angle, it is always possible therefore, to construct one from the other.

The principle governing inclined planes is similar to that governing inclined lines. Planes inclined to the ground have Vanishing Points above or below the Horizon Line, occurring in axes perpendicular to it.

In freehand drawing, inclined lines can be related to vertical planes or grids of the required proportion. Once the angles have been found, lines can be extended to meet the axis of the plane to produce the Vanishing Points. Any number of lines or planes inclined to the same angle can be constructed from the same VP.

Inclined planes reproduced in perspective by relating them to a perspective grid.

98

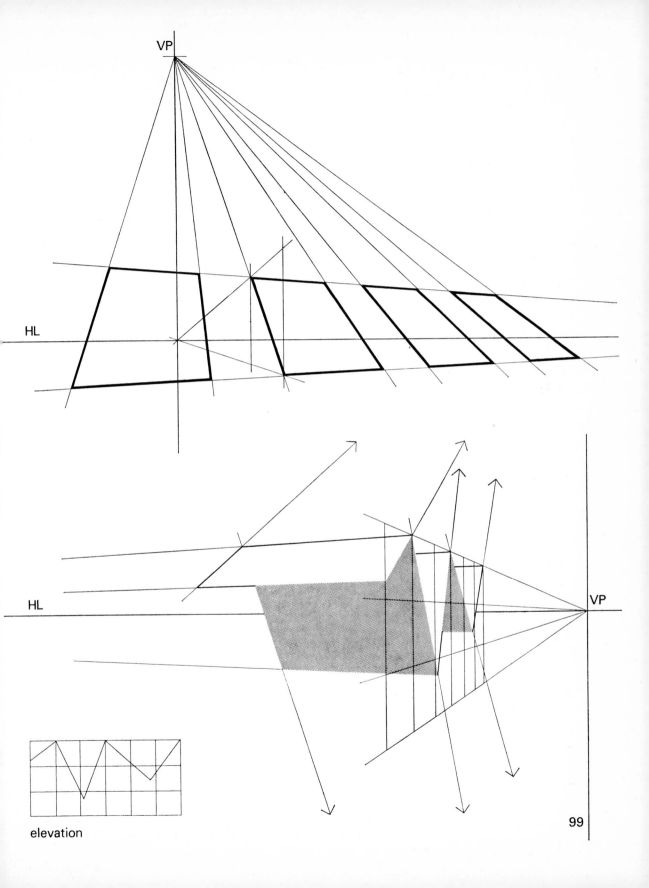

VP

HL

HL

VP

elevation

99

Curved Lines and Planes

A curved line reproduced in perspective by relating it to a perspective grid.

A curved line can be reproduced in perspective by relating it to a rectangular grid. Cartesian coordinates superimposed on the plan, are reproduced in perspective, and their intersections with the curved line plotted out. The curved line can then be drawn in perspective, through the points of intersection.

A height-plane is required to convert the curved line into a plane. From a vertical height-plane erected on one side of the base grid, a series of perpendicular planes are extended to meet the curved line. The top vertices of the planes reproduce the corresponding points on the curve, so that when connected, they complete the curved plane in perspective.

Perpendicular planes projected from a height-plane, can also be constructed at random points on a curved line, without the use of a grid.

Perpendicular planes projected from a base line to reproduce the top edge of a curved plane.

100

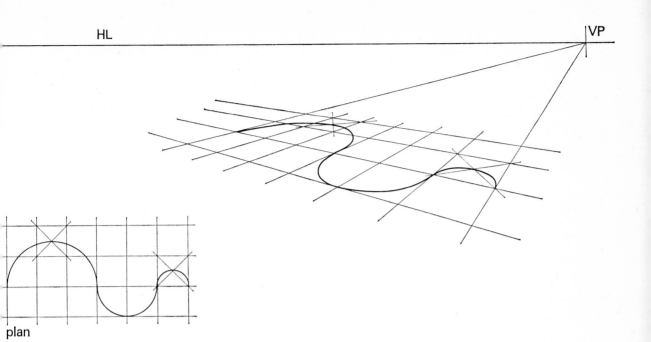

HL   VP

plan

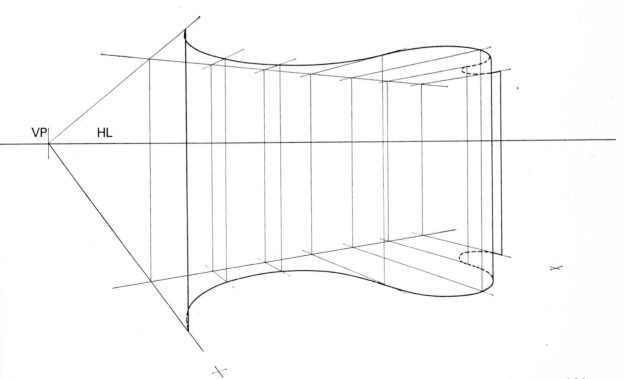

VP   HL

Arcs

Lines connecting points a, c and b, d give tangents of an arc centred on the opposite vertex of the square.

Intersections of lines ab with cd, and ef with gh produce points lying in an arc centred on the opposite vertex of the square.

Numerous techniques have been used to relate the circle to the square in order that it may be easily reproduced in perspective. The examples given here have a similar application, but they are shown principally because of their mathematical interest. All the constructions can be carried out directly on the perspective drawing.

If a square is divided along two adjacent edges into halves and thirds, lines connecting these points can be drawn to give tangents of an arc centred on the opposite vertex. The points of contact between the arc and tangents, occur at a distance of one fifth in from the outside edges of the square. This same relationship can be found when a semi-circle is inscribed in a $\sqrt{4}$ rectangle.

A square divided along its edges into 30 units contains two right-angled triangles of 3, 4, 5 ratio; the vertices of the angles opposite the long sides lie in an arc contained by the square.

Points in an arc contained by a square determined by the vertices of two right-angled triangles with edges in ratio of 3, 4, 5.

The intersection of a semi-circle inscribed in a $\sqrt{4}$ rectangle with a diagonal produces a ratio of 4 : 1 on adjacent edges.

102

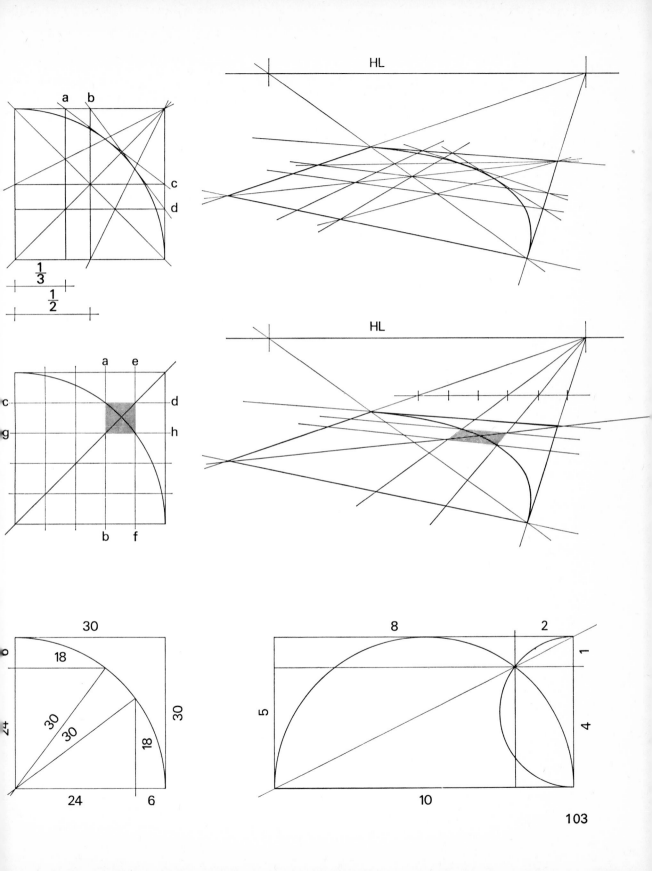

Helices

A helix in perspective constructed from the vertices of a series of vertical planes radiating from a common centre.

A helix can be drawn in perspective by connecting the top vertices of a series of vertical planes, radiating from a common centre and increasing in height as they progress. For convenience, the planes can be located on the diagonals and major axes of a square, forming eight segments on plan.

Draw a square in perspective, and construct an ellipse so that it touches the centres of its sides. Extend the diagonals of the square to find the Points of Distance in the Horizon Line. These points together with the VPs will serve as a guide for all subsequent lines.

Erect a perpendicular from the mid-point of the square, and graduate as a Height Line.

Draw the first vertical plane in perspective at one unit in height, and proceed with successive planes in order, taking the height from the central Height Line, and the length, from the intersection of the plane with the ellipse. The helix is drawn by joining the outer top vertices of each plane with a suitably curved line. Since the helix lies on the surface of a cylinder described by the ellipse, its path must at all times be contained within it.

Secondary lines at one unit down from the top of each vertical plane can be added, to form the risers of a spiral staircase. The steps are then filled in as segments of ellipses which become flattened out as they approach the level of the Horizon.

The steps of a spiral staircase in perspective form a series of segments of arcs which flatten out as they approach the level of the Horizon.

104

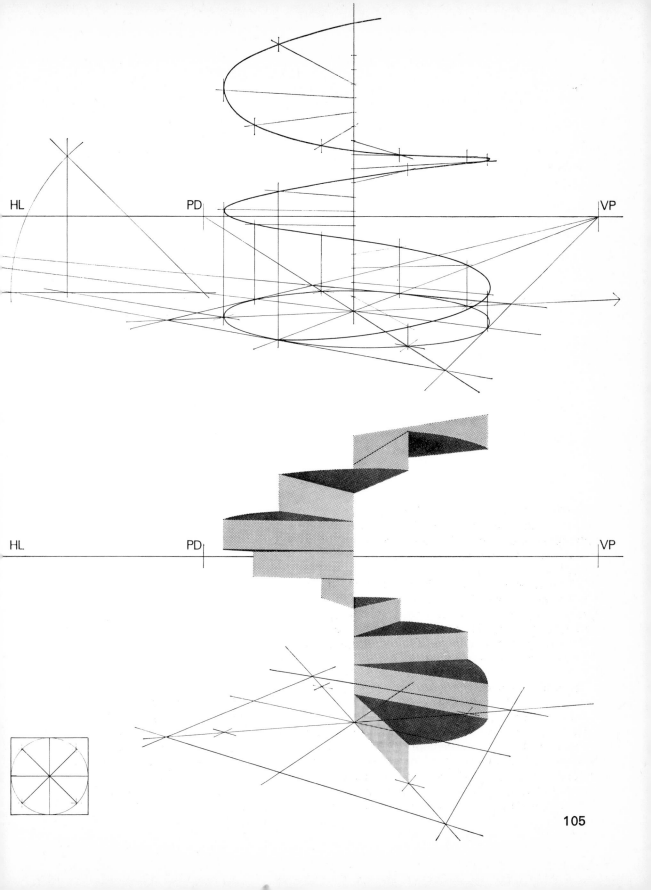

HL

PD

VP

HL

PD

VP

105

Spheres

Spheres in measured perspective.

A sphere can be imagined as a figure of rotation formed by an infinite number of concentric circular planes.

A sphere sits exactly within a Cube, its surface touching the centres of the six faces. In perspective the sphere is subject to the same degree of distortion as the Cube, but due to its form this is much less obvious.

From whatever angle a sphere is observed, there will always be one plane at right-angles to the visual ray passing through its centre ; this plane, subject to minor distortion, will appear to be circular. For all practical purposes a sphere can be represented as a circle in perspective, and can be drawn with a pair of compasses. It remains necessary to find its correct centre and relative scale of magnitude.

In measured perspective only the centres of spheres need be projected to the Picture Plane. Height Lines are taken vertically from the centres of the spheres on plan to intercept the Ground Line, and height planes projected forwards in perspective from the Point of Sight. Visual rays from the Observer give the length of the height planes, and from these are obtained the centres of the spheres in perspective.

The centre of the circle, used to represent a sphere in perspective, occurs at the true centre of any elliptical Great Circle plane which it contains, and not at the perspective centre of the enveloping Cube. The radius of the circle is half the length of the major axis of the ellipse.

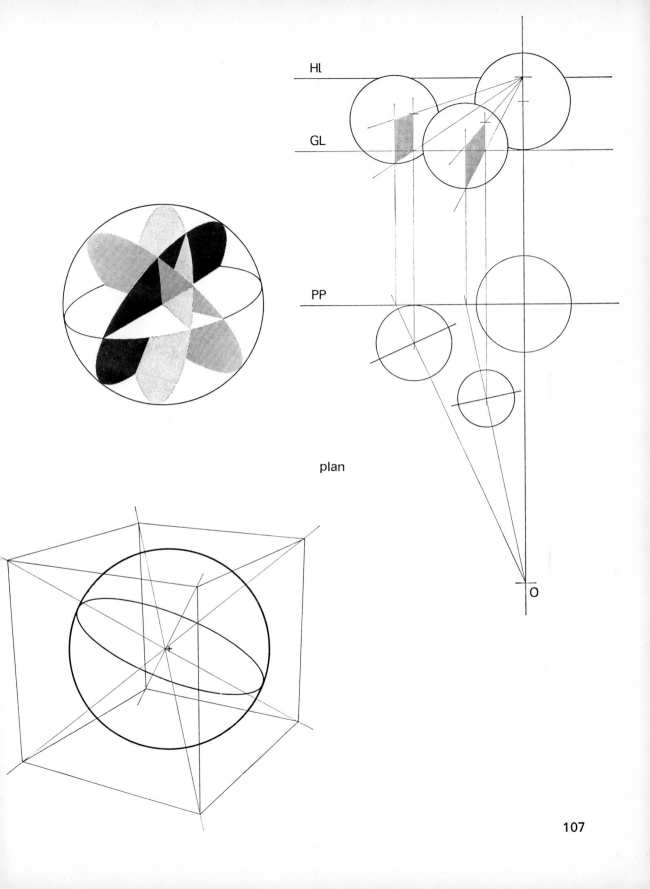

HI

GL

PP

plan

O

Methods of Enlargement and Diminution

PDs located in the centre of the figure used to diminish it.

PD located in the vertex of a figure used to enlarge or diminish it.

Radial lines from a Point of Distance, passing through all points on the drawing, can be used for the purpose of enlarging or diminishing. Lines parallel with those on the original drawing are constructed at the required distance from the PD to intersect the radials, thus forming a duplication of the outline to a different scale. The Point of Distance can be placed anywhere on the drawing, but conversion of the scale is made easier if it is located in an outside edge or vertex.

Triangulation can be used as an alternative means of converting one scale to another. Additional lines are added to the original drawing, as necessary, to form a completely triangulated net. The whole is then redrawn to the required scale by the use of an adjustable set-square. Since all angles remain constant, all measurements remain in proportion to each other as the whole is enlarged or diminished. Any edge, or any two points, on the original network can be used as a basis for commencement, and for conversion of the scale.

A logarithmic spiral enlarged or diminished by a PD. In this case the PD corresponds with the point of origin of the spiral.

Lines ab, bc, cd, etc., are drawn parallel to a^1b^1, b^1c^1, c^1d^1, etc., or vice versa.

The triangulated figure of the Stella Octangular can be redrawn, to any scale, by keeping all angles constant with the original.

108

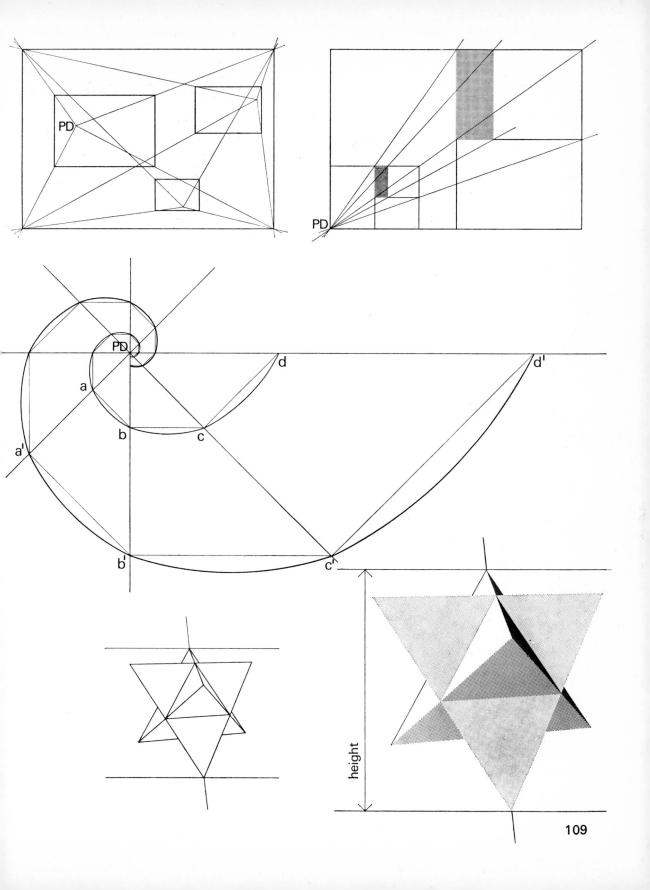

Projective Geometry

Desargues' Theorem

'If two triangles are perspective from a point, they are perspective from a line, and conversely.' Gérard Desargues proved the possibility of theorems of projection, completely independent of Euclidean geometry. He showed that in projection, the relative positions of points on a straight line are preserved when different angles and different ratios are used. The essential symmetry of this theorem is clearly demonstrated when considered three-dimensionally instead of as a flat diagram.

On the Tetrahedron OABC mark any three points A'B'C', A' on OA, B' on OB and C' on OC. Extend AB and A'B' to meet at Y, BC and B'C' to meet at Z, and AC and A'C' to meet at X. It will be found that the points XYZ lie in a straight line. The same result is produced when the Tetrahedron is not regular, and when the triangle A¹ B¹ C¹ occurs at any vertex, and at any angle.

Pascal's Mystic Hexagon

In another theorem, Blaise Pascal proved that if any hexagon is inscribed in a conic section, e.g. an ellipse, or circle in perspective, the three points of intersection of pairs of opposite sides are colinear. This theorem was later dualized by Charles Brianchon, who proved that if a hexagon is circum-scribed about a conic, its three diagonals are concurrent.

The three points of intersection of pairs of opposite sides of a hexagon, inscribed in a conic section, lie in a straight line.

Cross-ratio

The cross-ratio, expressed as (ABCD), of any four points lying in a straight line represents a single number. This number remains unchanged when the line is reproduced in perspective.

$$x = \frac{(a-b)(c-d)}{(b-c)(d-a)}$$

ABCD are set out at equal distances on the Ground Line, and lines extended through them to a Vanishing Point. A line is then drawn from a second VP to intersect the convergent lines at A'B'C'D' thus reproducing the original points in perspective. In the example given, the distances from A, using A as point of origin, are A $= 0$, AB $= 10$, AC $= 20$, and AD $= 30$. The distances from A' are A' $= 0$, A'B' $= 1$, A'C' $= 3$, and A'D' $= 9$. The cross-ratios for ABCD and A'B'C'D' are equal.

$$\frac{(0-10)(20-30)}{(10-20)(30-0)} = \frac{1}{-3}$$

$$\frac{(0-1)(3-9)}{(1-3)(9-0)} = \frac{1}{-3}$$

The cross-ratios,
$$x = \frac{(a-b)(c-d)}{(b-c)(d-a)}$$
for ABCD and A'B'C'D' are equal in perspective.

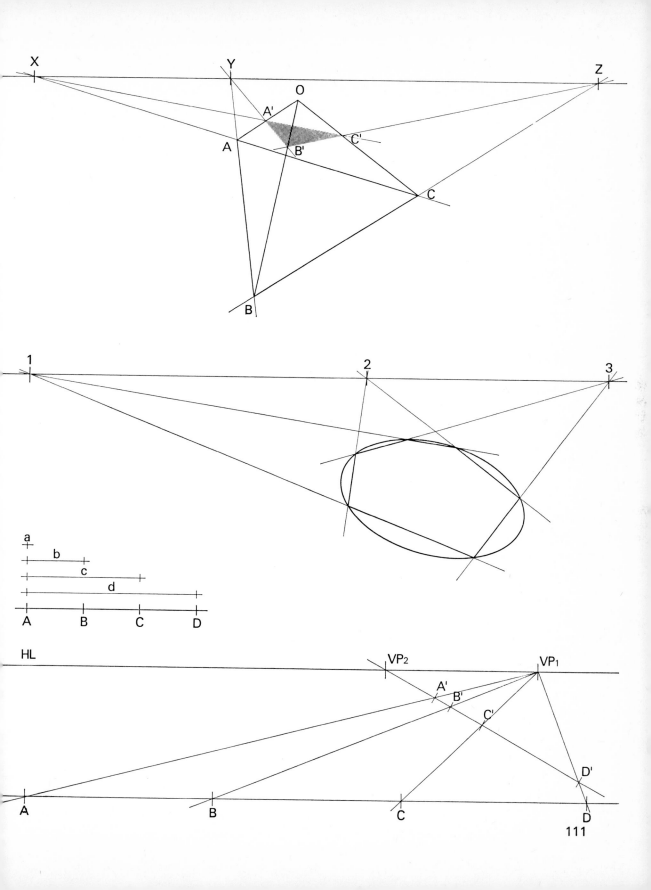

Regular and Semi-Regular Solids

A regular solid or polyhedron, may be defined as a finite connected set of plane polygons, such that every side of each polygon belongs also to one other polygon. The polygons are called faces and their sides edges, the points formed by their angles are called vertices. The vertices of all regular and semi-regular solids lie on the surface of a sphere, as also do the centres of their edges. Semi-regular solids have faces of more than one type of polygon.

There are five regular and thirteen semi-regular solids. The five regular solids, known as the Platonic bodies, are:

	faces	vertices	edges	edges per face
Tetrahedron	4	4	6	3
Cube	6	8	12	4
Octahedron	8	6	12	3
Icosahedron	20	12	30	3
Dodecahedron	12	20	30	5

Duality

Every polyhedron can be reciprocated with respect to a sphere, the centres of faces of one figure becoming the vertices of another 'dual' polyhedron, with its numbers of faces and vertices interchanged. The Octahedron and Cube are reciprocal, as are the couple Icosahedron and Dodecahedron. The Tetrahedron is said to be auto-reciprocal because its centres of faces describe a second, smaller, figure of the same form.

Tetrahedron

The edges of the Tetrahedron correspond with the diagonals of the faces of a Cube.

Octahedron

The vertices of the Octahedron occur at the centres of faces of a Cube.

The centres of faces, centres of edges and vertices of a regular polyhedron lie on the surfaces of three concentric spheres — the Insphere, the Intersphere, and the Circumsphere. For a cube edge 2, successive radii of the Insphere, Intersphere, and Circumsphere are 1, $\sqrt{2}$, and $\sqrt{3}$; successive diameters are $\sqrt{4}$, $\sqrt{8}$, and $\sqrt{12}$.

Radii of the Insphere, Intersphere and Circumsphere located in the diagonal plane of a Cube. Octahedron as dual of Cube.

Tetrahedron and dual.

Octahedron as dual of Cube.

112

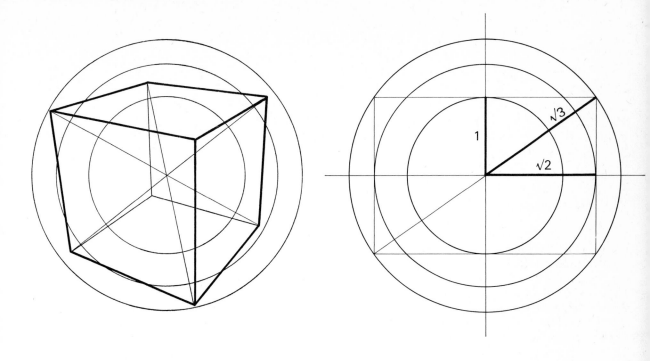

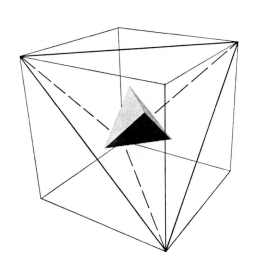

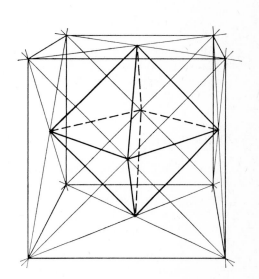

Icosahedron

The diameter of the intersphere of the Icosahedron is Φ when the edge is 1, it can be constructed from three intersecting Golden Section rectangles arranged on the major axes of a Cube.

Draw a Cube in perspective and divide the faces diagonally to find the centres. Construct a $\sqrt{4}$ rectangle, or double square, on one of the uprights so that the Φ ratio can be obtained from its diagonal, and set this out above and below the centre line to give the proportion 0·618 : 1 : 1 : 0·618. Convey this proportion to one of the central axes using the Vanishing Point and complete the first Φ rectangle in perspective. Repeat for the other two axes using a diagonal to convey the proportion from one face to another. Join the vertices of the three intersecting Φ rectangles in sets of three to produce the twenty triangular faces of the Icosahedron.

Alternatively, the Fibonacci Series can be used to establish the Golden Section ratio. Divide the Cube edge to the ratio 3 : 5 : 5 : 3, or 5 : 8 : 8 : 5, etc.

Three intersecting Golden Section rectangles constructed within a Cube.

Icosahedron derived from the vertices of three intersecting Φ rectangles. In Triaxial Perspective, ratio obtained from consecutive terms in the Fibonacci Series set out on a Measuring Line and used with a Point of Distance.

Dodecahedron

Eight of the vertices of the Dodecahedron correspond with the vertices of a Cube ; the Cube edges forming chords of the twelve pentagonal faces. The diameter of the intersphere of the Dodecahedron is 2·618 when the edge is 1, and the edge of the circumscribed Cube is Φ.

Proceed as for the Icosahedron and extend the three intersecting planes by the addition of $\sqrt{4}$ rectangles, or double squares. These can be produced by using the PD for the semidiagonal of each face of the Cube. Connect the vertices of the extended planes with the vertices of the Cube, to obtain the Dodecahedron.

Dodecahedron derived from the vertices of three intersecting Φ + 1 rectangles and the vertices of a Cube.

114

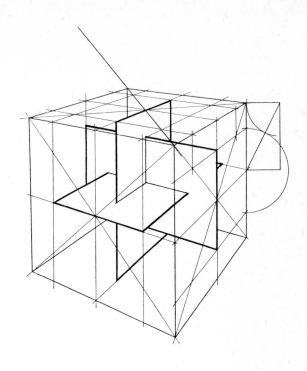

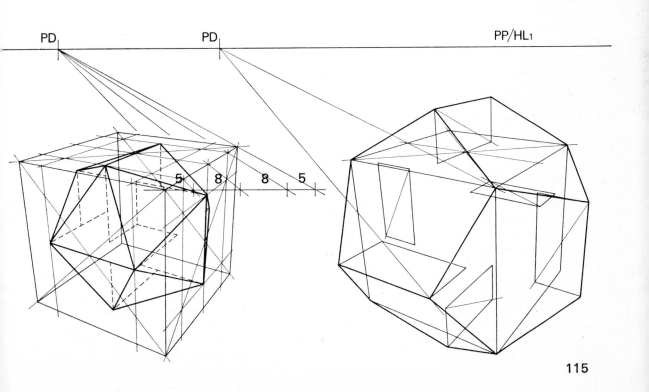

Cuboctahedron

The semi-regular, Cuboctahedron, has the six square faces of the Cube and the eight triangular faces of the Octahedron. It is formed by the centres of edges of the Cube, and will close-pack space in association with an equal number of Octahedra.

In the Cuboctahedral close-packing of spheres each sphere is surrounded by twelve others, their centres corresponding with the vertices of the Cuboctahedron.

Cuboctahedron.
f : 14   v : 12   e : 24

Tetrakaidecahedron

The Tetrakaidecahedron, or truncated Octahedron, in common with the Cube, is capable of close-packing space in a three-dimensional tessellation using units only of its own kind. Six of its faces are coplanar with the faces of a Cube.

Tetrakaidecahedron.
f : 14   v : 24   e : 36

Rhombic Dodecahedron

The Rhombic Dodecahedron, dual of the Cuboctahedron, can be formed by the radii or semi-diagonals of eight small Cubes arranged to form a larger Cube. Six of its vertices lie on the face of the larger Cube and describe an Octahedron, the remaining eight vertices describe a small Cube. It will fill space itself by repetition.

Rhombic Dodecahedron.
f : 12   v : 14   e : 24

Stellated Rhombic Dodecahedron

The Stellated Rhombic Dodecahedron or 'Mystic Star', can be formed by the diagonals of eight small Cubes arranged to form a larger Cube. Eighteen of its vertices and twenty-four of its edges, lie on the face of the larger Cube ; the remaining eight vertices describe a small Cube. It will fill space itself by repetition.

Stellated Rhombic Dodecahedron.

The regular partitioning of space

The Cube and Truncated Octahedron, are the only regular, or semi-regular, solids which can be close-packed in space without leaving intervals. Other solids capable of close-filling space with members of their own kind, include the Rhombic Dodecahedron and the Triangular and Hexagonal Prisms. Isotropic point-lattices: lattices with equal distances between neighbouring points, can be formed by Tetrahedra and Octahedra in the ratio of two to one, or by Cuboctahedra and Octahedra in equal numbers.

Isotropic point-lattices are composed of seven sets of intersecting planes, four comprising triangular grids or tessellations, and three square tessellations : the axial planes correspond in both form and arrangement with the faces of the Cuboctahedron. Any two successive grids from the lattice define what is termed a Double-layer Grid Structure.

116

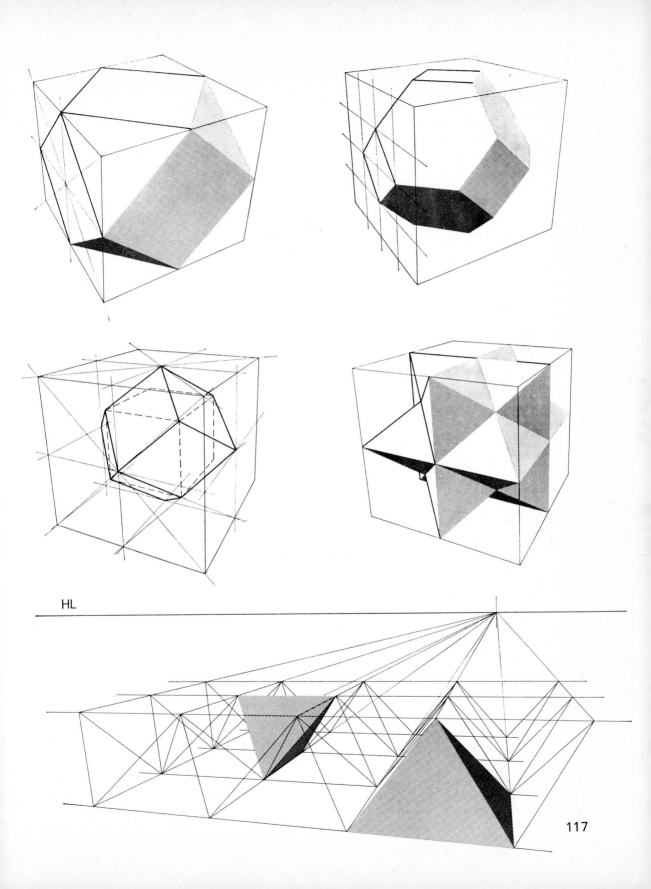

HL

Orthographic Projection

First Angle Projection, European Standard excluding Dutch projection. Each view shows what would be seen by looking on the far side of an adjacent view.

Orthographic projection is the representation of an object by means of a scale plan and elevations, it is described as First, or Third Angle Projection, depending on the arrangement of the elevations with respect to the plan. The revised British Standard Projection for architects and builders, Recommendations for Building Drawing Practice, Metric Units. BS 1192 : 1969, is first angle projection ; that for Engineering Drawing Practice, BS 308 :1964, accepts both first and third angle projection. Elevations not square with the plan are projected at right-angles to their surface so that they remain true to scale, these are described as True Projections.

Elevations of interiors are generally referred to as Sections since they represent sections through the plan, their positions on plan are indicated by break lines denoted A-A, B-B, etc. For convenience in reading, sections are sometimes set out in rows independently of the plan.

All parts of the drawing should be properly identified either with descriptive notes or with joined projection lines.

Third Angle Projection, American and Dutch projection. Each view shows what would be seen by looking on the near side of an adjacent view.

Combination of First and Third Angle Projection, used by Architects and Builders.

First and Third Angle Projection conform with British Standard for Engineering Drawing Practice.

118

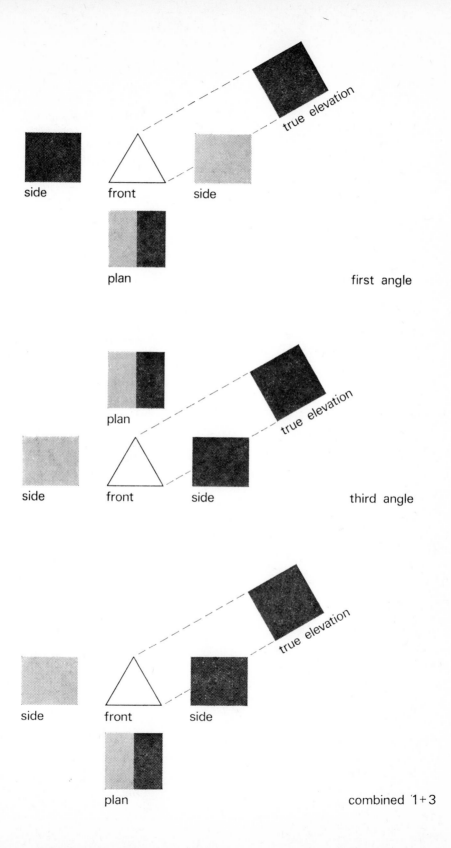

side   front   side   true elevation

plan

first angle

plan

side   front   side   true elevation

third angle

side   front   side   true elevation

plan

combined 1+3

*First Angle and Third Angle projections
are conventions for setting out drawings. First and Third refer to two of the
four dihedral angles formed by the
intersection of a vertical and a
horizontal plane; the common notation
being as illustrated.*

*The object is viewed either in First or
Third Angle always from above and
from the right. Lines are projected
backwards or forwards from the object
to the relevant planes, and the planes
are then opened out to form a flat
drawing.
The order becomes:
First Angle; Observer, object, plane of
projection.
Third Angle; Observer, plane of projection, object.*

*First Angle Projection, planes folded
flat.*

*Third Angle Projection, planes folded
flat.*

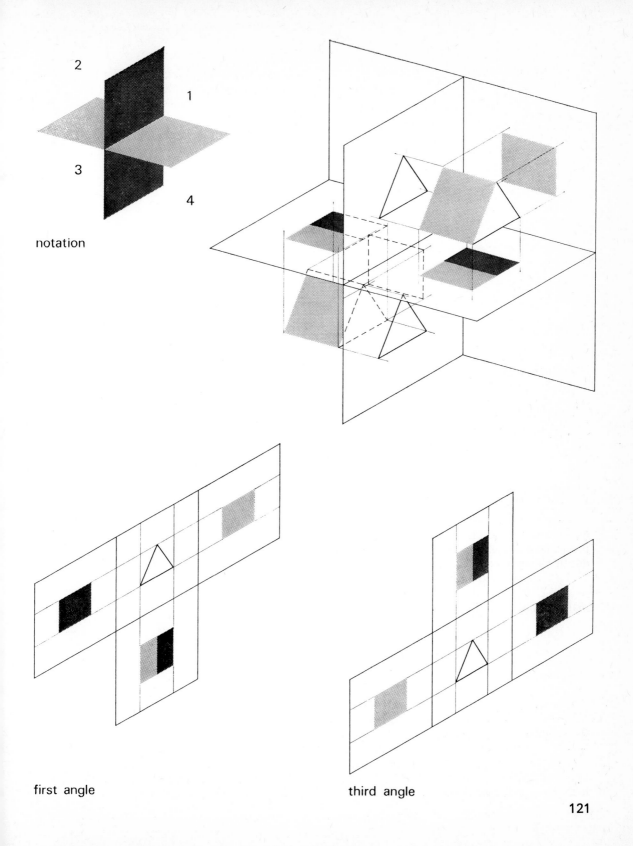

2

1

3

4

notation

first angle

third angle

121

Parallel Projection

Oblique projection, 1 : 1 : 1 sometimes termed Cavalier.

Oblique projection, 2 : 2 : 1 sometimes termed Cabinet.

Parallel projections offer a suitable alternative to perspective for technical illustrations and diagrams where dimensions have to be given, they can be constructed entirely with the aid of a set-square and scale rule.

Oblique Projection

Oblique projection is a modified form of scale elevation where return planes on two sides are projected obliquely. Dimensions of height, width and depth, can either remain constant in the ratio of 1 : 1 : 1, or adjusted to give greater realism in the ratio of 2 : 2 : 1. Circles and arcs lying in the return planes become elliptical.

Planometric projection, 1 : 1 : 1.

Planometric Projection

Planometric projection is a modified form of scale plan where the plan is rotated to a suitable angle and the elevations projected vertically. Dimensions of height, width and depth, can either remain constant in the ratio of 1 : 1 : 1, or adjusted to give greater realism in the ratio of 1 : 2 : 2. Circles and arcs lying in the vertical planes become elliptical.

Planometric with reduced vertical scale, sometimes referred to as Military Perspective, 1 : 2 : 2.

122

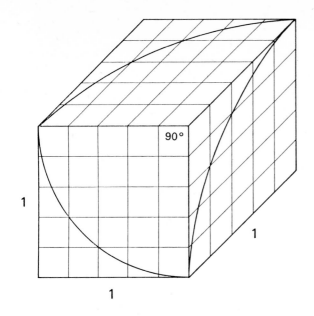

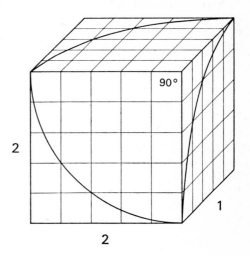

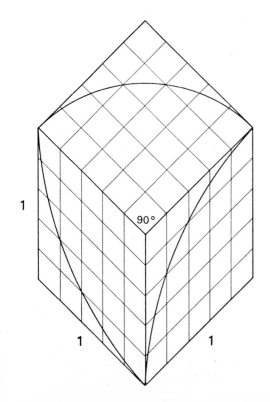

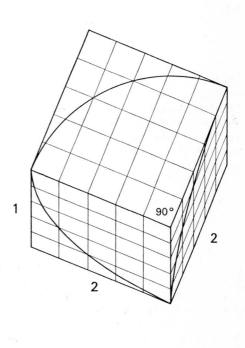

Axonometric Projection

Axonometric is a generic term for any projected view of an object in which the projectors are perpendicular to the plane of projection, and the three faces of the object are all inclined to the plane of projection.

Isometric Projection

Isometric projection is a form of Axonometric where the plan is flattened so that the face angles of a square become 120° and 60°. Dimensions of height, width and depth remain constant in the ratio of 1 : 1 : 1. All circles and arcs lying in the faces of a Cube become elliptical.

Isometric projection, 1 : 1 : 1.

Dimetric Projection

Dimetric projection is a modified form of Isometric where any two dimensions of height, width or depth, are adjusted to give greater realism, usually in the ratio of 2 : 2 : 1, or 3 : 3 : 1. All circles and arcs lying in the faces of a Cube become elliptical.

Dimetric projection, 2 : 2 : 1.
In Dimetric Projection there are two scales of dimensions for edges and two angles of faces for the Cube.

Trimetric Projection

Trimetric projection is a further modification of Isometric where all three dimensions of height, width and depth, are adjusted, usually in the ratio of 6 : 5 : 4 or 10 : 9 : 5. All circles and arcs lying in the faces of a Cube become elliptical.

Trimetric projection, 6 : 5 : 4
In Trimetric projection there are three scales of dimensions for edges and three angles of faces for the Cube.

In Dimetric and Trimetric projection the angles subtended at the vertex of a Cube are determined by the angles of rotation and tilt and are directly related to the relative lengths of edges of the Cube in projection.

Exploded Views

In exploded views, separated component parts of a figure are projected in such a way that they retain their original relationship with each other and with the major axes on which they lie. Exploded views are used in engineering and product design to show how an article is manufactured or how it is assembled. The technique can be applied equally well in either parallel projection or perspective. Broken lines are used to indicate the movement of the pieces.

Exploded view of a three-burr construction.

124

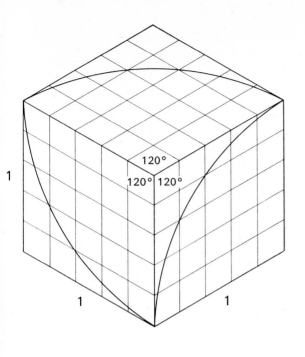

120°
120° 120°

1

1   1

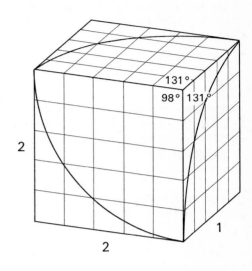

131°
98° 131°

2

2   1

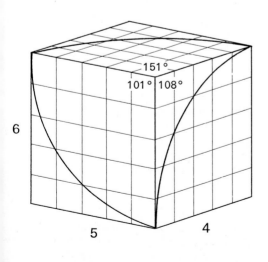

151°
101° 108°

6

5   4

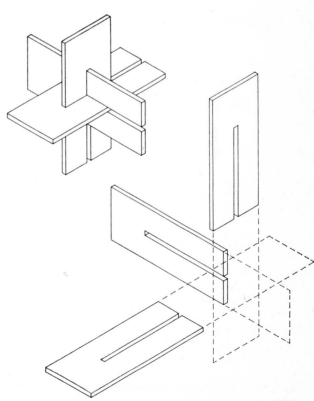

Definitions

Aerial Perspective. Non-linear perspective in which changes in tone and colour occur as objects recede due to atmospheric density; contrasts become muted and colours tend towards blue.

Angle of Vision. The angle subtended at O by visual rays from the object's edge.

Angular Perspective. Projection using two or more Vanishing Points. Adjacent faces of a Cube in Angular Perspective converge to Vanishing Points on either side of the Centre of Vision.

Axis, axes. Imaginary line about which a given body or system rotates. Axis of Symmetry, the central axis of a symmetrical body or figure. Perspective axis, a line or plane in which related Vanishing Points or Points of Distance occur.

Axonometric. A generic term for some parallel projections.

Centre of Vision. CV. Central visual plane passing from the Observer to the object.

Central Visual Ray. Central axis of the Cone of Vision.

Coaxial. Lying in the same axis.

Cone of Vision. The cone bounded by the eye of the Observer at its apex and by the Field of Vision at its base.

Colinear. Lying in the same line.

Coordinates. A precise reference framework to locate a point, line, or plane in two- or three-dimensional space. First conceived by Descartes and developed by Leibniz, the axes *x, y, z,* are used to express the concept of width, height, and depth. By this system a circle can be described in the form $r^2 = x^2 + y^2$.

Coplanar. Lying in the same plane.

Elevation. Scale drawing in vertical projection.

Enantiomorphic. A left hand and right hand pair each being a mirror image of the other, for example the left and right hand helices of a ram's horns.

Eye Level. Fixed plane at the Observer's eye-height. In perspective it coincides with the Horizon Line where the two surfaces, Eye Plane and Terrestrial Plane, appear to meet.

Field of Vision. The area of the object in sharp focus to the Observer and encompassed by the Cone of Vision.

Foot of the Luminary. FTL. Vanishing Point for shadows. The FTL lies in the vertical axis of the luminary and is generally found in the Horizon Line when shadows are cast by the sun.

Great Circle. Line produced on the surface of a sphere when cut by a plane passing through its centre.

Ground Line. GL. Base of the Picture Plane in perspective. The vertical distance of the GL from the Horizon Line is determined by the eye-height of the Observer.

Height Line. Line used for vertical measurements. In measured perspective the Height Line occurs at any point where the plan is intersected by the Picture Plane.

Horizon Line. HL. Visual boundary of the Ground or Terrestrial Plane. In perspective the HL always appears at the Observer's eye-height.

Isometric. Parallel projection in which the edges of a Cube are of equal measure and the angles of faces are 120° and 60°.

Measuring Line. ML. Ground Line in Triaxial perspective. The vertical distance between HL and ML corresponds with the distance between the eye-plane of the Observer and the Point of Sight.

Measuring Point. MP. A point found in the Picture Plane and Horizon Line used for conveying dimensions from the Ground Line or Measuring Line to points in perspective.

Oblique Perspective. Perspective in which no two sides of a Cube remain parallel; also termed Three Point, and Triaxial perspective.

Oblique Projection. A form of parallel projection.

Observer. O. Point of the Observer on plan corresponding with the point of origin of the visual rays.

Orthographic Projection. Parallel projection of plans and elevations in which all angles remain constant and all dimensions true to scale.

Parallel Perspective. Projection using one principal Vanishing Point. In Parallel Perspective two sets of planes, usually the vertical and horizontal, remain parallel.

Picture Plane. PP. Imaginary plane used in measured perspective; it is the focal plane onto which all information is projected, and it appears on plan as a straight line perpendicular to the Centre of Vision.

Plan. Scale drawing of the object viewed from above. In measured perspective it includes the position of the Observer and the Picture Plane.

Plane of Light. In shadow projection, a plane perpendicular to the ground extending from the Point of Distance for the luminary and the Foot of the Luminary, through any point on the object.

Plane of Shade. Area of the Plane of Light obscured by the object and forming a triangle with the ground to define the length of shadow.

Point of Distance. PD. Vanishing Point for construction lines. PDL., Point of Distance for the luminary.

Point of Sight. PS. Intersection of coordinate planes CV and HL. In Parallel Perspective, it corresponds with the Central Vanishing Point.

Polygon. Many-sided plane figure with straight edges. Regular polygon, figure having equal sides and equal angles.

Polyhedron, polyhedra. Three-dimensional solid with polygonal faces.

Sciagraphy. Shadow projection.

Seat of the Sun's Rays. Vanishing Point for shadows, also termed Foot of the Luminary.

Small Circle. Circle formed on the surface of a sphere when cut by a plane which does not pass through its centre.

Symmetry. Exact correspondence in size and shape between opposite sides of a figure. Dynamic Symmetry, visual balance of geometrical or mathematical origin as found in the Golden Section ratio.

Terrestrial Plane. Ground plane extending from the Observer to the Horizon.

Trapezium. Any quadrilateral especially one with two sides parallel.

Triaxial Perspective. Projection using three or more Vanishing Points in which no two sides of a Cube remain parallel.

Trompe L'Oeil. The representation on a flat surface of persons or objects in three dimensions to give an illusion of reality.

Vanishing Parallel. Van. Par. In measured perspective a line drawn on plan from the Observer to the Picture Plane parallel with the sides of the object. Used to determine the position of Vanishing Points in the Picture Plane.

Vanishing Point. VP. A point in the Horizon Line, or other axis, at which parallel lines appear to meet in perspective.

Vertex, vertices. The point produced by the intersection of adjacent edges of a plane figure or geometrical solid